Twayne's United States Authors Series

Sylvia E. Bowman, *Editor*

INDIANA UNIVERSITY

William Gilmore Simms

WILLIAM GILMORE SIMMS

by J. V. RIDGELY

Columbia University

(TUSAS) 28

Twayne Publishers, Inc.   ::   New York

To Janetta

Preface

OF WILLIAM GILMORE SIMMS in the year of his death (1870), Allibone's *Dictionary* said: "One of the most voluminous and popular of American authors." Since Simms had published more than eighty volumes, as well as a mass of miscellaneous periodical literature, no one could challenge the accuracy of the first part of Allibone's comment. But Simms's popularity was already waning after the Civil War, and only a fraction of his works can be found in twentieth-century reprints. It is true that in 1892 he achieved inclusion among the writers memorialized in the old American Men of Letters series, and since that date he has usually been accorded notice in standard literary histories and anthologies. He has, further, been the subject of several unpublished academic dissertations; and occasional scholarly articles have examined various facets of his long career. The five hefty volumes of his letters, issued 1952-56, stirred up some new interest, for they provided the first ample and accurate framework for judging the man and the writer. Yet, on the whole, the modern reader's acquaintance with Simms is still apt to be confined to one book—his early romance of Indian warfare, *The Yemassee*, recently reprinted in Twayne's United States Classics Series. This study is the first published one to survey at length a significant body of Simms's writing.

It is not difficult to determine why Simms has not attracted more general attention. To begin with, the canon of his work in several fields is truly formidable; according to the tabulation of one collector, A. S. Salley, his eighty-two books included thirty-four works of fiction, nineteen volumes of poetry, three of drama, three anthologies, three volumes of history, two of geography, six biographies, and twelve gatherings of reviews, miscellanies, and addresses. In addition, he left many other tales, poems, reviews, and essays scattered through a host of Southern and Northern periodicals. But nearly all of these works have long been out of print and are now impossible to obtain even from rare-book dealers. The only collected edition—the twenty selected volumes of fiction and poetry published in the 1850's (and reprinted several times from the same plates)—is also hard to purchase, though it may be consulted in some university and public libraries. The sheer bulk of his work and the difficulty of locating it today have made Simms troublesome to know.

Simms, moreover, was particularly unfortunate in having William P. Trent assigned as his first biographer and critic. For Trent, a fervent proponent of the "New South" movement of his day, had as his subject a man who for a lifetime had championed a diametrically opposed ideal. Not surprisingly, Trent's 1892 study in the American Men of Letters series appraised Simms and his output against the background of a primitive and retrogressive Old South. In the biographer's eyes, the South that Simms had made the subject of much of his fiction was a loathsome, discredited region—a would-be nation that had quite justly been toppled in war. It followed, to Trent, that since Simms had lived under the blight of a slave system, his writings inevitably lacked the "nobility" and "uplift" to which only art produced within a free society could aspire. Throughout the biography run pejorative epithets which betray the critic's bias: "low," "repulsive," "horrible," "unnatural," and "uncalled for."

Trent insisted, too, that Simms had never really been accepted by the snobbish Charleston ruling classes, and he implied that Simms erred fatally as a novelist by trying to woo them with Southern tales which reflected their prejudices. This belief drove Trent to the untenable position of praising some of Simms's works about other subjects simply because he found in them a higher "moral" tone. His book is still useful since it contains data unobtainable elsewhere; but the effect of its persuasive rhetoric has been to keep many critics from ever inquiring beyond the judgments Trent made upon Simms.

In 1927 Vernon L. Parrington, in the second volume of *Main Currents in American Thought*, partially qualified Trent's views; but Parrington's own devotion to social realism led to equally slanted conclusions. Unlike some other commentators, Parrington actually read a number of Simms's books, and he rated their author as "by far the most virile and interesting figure of the Old South." His critique, however, was warped by the notion that Simms was fundamentally a realist in the Fielding-Smollett vein who was restrained by his environment from ever giving full and free expression to his native talents. Simms had lived, he decided, in "a world of unreality, of social and economic romanticism, that was forever benumbing his strong instinct for reality."

These two studies—Trent's and Parrington's—have long been echoed by other critics. Both men built upon a basic assumption that Simms as a writer had been stultified by the Old South—and their estimate still has its adherents. My own analysis takes exactly the opposite view, and it is only fair to inform the reader of my position at the start. My central thesis is that Simms was devoted throughout his career to the theme of the nature of Southern society; that his creativity was stimulated by this theme; and that in all his works which have literary merit the concept of the South as a unique and potentially perfectible society is the central organizing principle. I have endeavored to show that Simms's attitude toward his region was that of the maker of a "myth"—that of the creator through fiction of the vision of an ideal Southern social structure. It is for this achievement alone, I hold, that Simms has present relevance. I have limited my study, consequently, to those works which most clearly render this primary theme; and I have reduced biographical, historical, and source materials to a minimum.

My discussion is organized in this manner: Chapter I examines Simms's personal relationship to his region, summarizes the general "myth" or legend of the South which he developed at length in his fiction, and surveys briefly the work of other Southern authors of the ante-bellum period. Chapter II considers Simms's definitions of the romance and the novel, indicates why he preferred the former genre, and notes the influences upon him of other romance writers. Chapters III-IX undertake a chronological, critical survey of those works of fiction by Simms which I have found most substantial. My plot summaries are occasionally more detailed than would be appropriate in a survey of a better-known author; I have felt it necessary to include them because of the general unavailability of many of the texts. In quoting from the Simms *Letters* and from his other writings, I have reproduced the originals exactly, except for an infrequent bracketed word of explanation or emendation. The reader will observe that Simms was not always consistent in his spelling and that he punctuated far more freely than modern practice dictates; it appeared pointless, however, to call attention to every error by a [*sic*].

I trust that I have not claimed for Simms any more than he genuinely merits. I readily concede that he wrote too much and too hastily and that even his most finished works never approach in style, structure, characterization, or insight the standards set by such contemporaries as Hawthorne and Melville. But if he is not an author of the first rank, he still has significance; and he does deserve a more just and detailed appraisal than earlier critics were willing to grant him. I hope only that my discussion will stimulate future readers to take a fresh look at the achievement of the most notable professional writer produced by the Old South.

J. V. RIDGELY

Columbia University

Acknowledgments

I am grateful to Mrs. Mary C. Simms Oliphant, granddaughter of Simms and co-editor of the five-volume *Letters of William Gilmore Simms* (University of South Carolina Press, 1952-56), for permission to make full use of this edition, the starting point for any investigation of Simms's life and works. I would like also to express my indebtedness to Professor Charles R. Anderson, of the Johns Hopkins University, who guided my original researches into Simms's fiction. The editors of *American Literature* have kindly consented to allow me to reprint portions of my article, "*Woodcraft:* Simms's First Answer to *Uncle Tom's Cabin,*" which appeared in the January, 1960, issue of that journal.

Nearly all of Simms's writings are currently out of print, and I have been aided in my attempts to find certain items by the staffs of several libraries. I would especially like to thank Miss Martha Hubbard, of the Johns Hopkins University Library staff; Mrs. G. Corner Fenhagen, of the Enoch Pratt Free Library of Baltimore; and the librarians of the Peabody Institute Library, the Library of Congress, and the Butler Library of Columbia University.

Contents

Chronology

1806   Born Charleston, South Carolina, April 17.

1808   Mother died; father moved to the Old Southwest; maternal grandmother took care of boy.

1824-1825   Visited father in Mississippi; traveled across lower South.

1825   First volume of verse; contributed to *The Album,* a Charleston periodical; studied law.

1826   Married Anna Malcolm Giles; one child, a daughter, born of this marriage.

1827   Admitted to the bar; second and third volumes of poetry, followed by two more in next three years.

1830-1832   Edited Charleston *City Gazette,* which opposed Nullification; was attacked by a mob for his political views.

1831   Second long tour through lower South.

1832   Death of wife; first visit to North, during which he met a number of literary figures; *Atalantis: A Story of the Sea.*

1833   *Martin Faber,* first extended work of fiction; *The Book of My Lady.*

1834   *Guy Rivers,* first of border romances.

1835   *The Yemassee,* first of colonial romances; *The Partisan,* first of Revolutionary War romances.

1836   Married Chevillette Eliza Roach; father-in-law owned "Woodlands" plantation in South Carolina, which became the Simms family home; *Mellichampe.*

1838   *Richard Hurdis.*

1840   *Border Beagles.*

1841   *The Kinsmen.*

1842   *Beauchampe.*

1844- Member of South Carolina legislature.
1846

1849- Edited *Southern Quarterly Review* (best of the several
1854 periodicals with which Simms was connected).

1850- Active exponent of secession.
1860

1851 *Katharine Walton.*

1852 *The Sword and the Distaff* (later retitled *Woodcraft*).

1853 Simms's New York publisher, J. S. Redfield, began publication of the "new and revised" edition of his works.

1855 *The Forayers.*

1856 *Eutaw;* a lecture tour in the North ended abruptly after Simms's pro-Southern remarks drew attacks.

1859 *The Cassique of Kiawah,* last romance in book form.

1862 "Woodlands" burned; public collection allowed restoration.

1863 Death of second wife, who had borne him fourteen children.

1865 "Woodlands" burned by stragglers from General Sherman's army; extensive library and art gallery destroyed.

1865- Turned out numerous stories, poems, and journalistic
1870 articles in effort to recoup losses and support family.

1870 Died Charleston, June 11.

William Gilmore Simms

CHAPTER 1

The Writer as Southerner

I *The Sense of Place*

NATHANIEL HAWTHORNE once observed, "New England is quite as large a lump of earth as my heart can really take in." His contemporary, William Gilmore Simms, put his own awareness of commitment to a region even more simply: "I am an ultra Southron." To Simms "the South" was infinitely more than a geographical designation for a group of states; the words stood for a nation within a nation—an area with a heroic past, a unique social structure, and a potentiality for an ideal future. These passionately held beliefs permeated all his best work; he suffered abuse for them in his lifetime, and critics have not yet entirely freed themselves from the prejudices—pro and con—which the words "the Old South" inevitably stir up in Americans.

Simms was born in Charleston, South Carolina, on April 17, 1806; with the exception of extensive tours of the lower South and occasional visits to his publishers in the North, he lived all his life within the confines of his native state. His family was already deeply rooted in the Southern soil by the year of his birth. His father had emigrated from Ireland some time after the American Revolution and had established himself as a Charleston merchant. His mother's family, the Singletons, had moved from Virginia to South Carolina even earlier; and all of them, Simms remarked proudly, "took a distinct part on the patriotic side in the struggle with the mother country."[1] Not much is known of Simms's Irish forebears, and he himself appears to have had little feeling for his European heritage. Even his own father remains an enigmatic figure. Exiling himself from Charleston after the death of his wife in 1808, the elder

Simms fought Indians under Andrew Jackson and eventually settled as a planter in frontier Mississippi; his son, the only issue of the marriage to survive, remembered him chiefly as a "discontented & forever wandering man" (*L*, I, 160).

The lonely boy was given over to the care of his maternal grandmother, a parsimonious woman, Simms later complained, who withheld the funds necessary for a thorough education (*L*, V, 357). But for the future historical romancer she supplied something more palatable than formal instruction since she delighted in spinning tales of the colonial settlement, of Indian warfare, and of the remembered days of the Revolution in the lower South.[2] Soon the youth, during his frequent bouts with sickness, was absorbing books of all sorts and weaving the fancies they stimulated into the sentimental, romantic verses which he was to gather in several of his early volumes.

Simms's boyhood rambles about Charleston, his wide reading, the yarns of his grandmother about the Southern past, and a visit to his father in Mississippi in 1824-25 all provided basic materials from which he was to create his long shelf of fiction. In later years he was to extend these resources by further travel, by involvement in local politics, by editing a number of Southern periodicals, and by serious historical research into the colonial and Revolutionary periods; always he was to remain most effective as a literary craftsman by keeping close to the topics which he knew from firsthand experience or from history and legend.

As the South in the 1850's plunged inexorably toward the Civil War, Simms became a recognized spokesman for its institutions; he could even welcome the war as signalizing the final break necessary for its future development as an entirely separate nation. The shock of defeat by the North, along with the many privations he had suffered, left him a broken man, physically and emotionally. He bowed to the military decision and tried to reconstruct his life and career in the five years that were left to him after 1865, but he could never concede that he had been wrong in his opinion that the South had been building toward an ideal society.

To understand the writings of Simms, then, it is necessary to take him for what at heart he was: a maker of myths about the South's past, present, and future during the important period when the area was seeking its identity. It must be said at once that many of his ideas—especially his insistence upon the South's God-given right to enslave other human beings—now violently repel most readers. It would be as foolish, though, for the literary critic to condemn Simms for his notions as it would be to chide an Elizabethan for belief in the divine right of kings; Simms was inescapably a child of his era and region. And yet the body of fiction which he produced is today as much a part of what Americans have imagined about themselves as is Hawthorne's vision of the Puritan past. Not only is it a record interesting in itself, for the way in which it reveals the essential mind of the South, but it may also help us better to understand the continuing power of the Old South legend over such modern writers as William Faulkner and Robert Penn Warren. Simms was never a great artist; but his achievement was a unique one, and it should no longer be slighted.

II *An Ordered Society*

As a Southerner and as a writer, Simms moved in the twin worlds of an actual South and a South of his imagination; he was practicing politician as well as poet and romancer. The practical side is the easier to consider first. Simms was a frequent critic of various characteristics of existing Southern society—its tendency toward luxury and lassitude, its lack of support for the arts, its self-seeking politicians, its wasteful use of the land, its economic weakness, its many other failures to live up to its capabilities.[3] But these criticisms were made out of a sense of sorrow and personal frustration and not out of any lasting disillusionment. To try to reconcile the tensions and the conflicts he observed in the world around him—the city, the plantation, and the frontier—he sought an ordering scheme, a plan by which society could settle itself and then advance toward perfection.

Early in his career Simms found a paradigm in the ancient concept of hierarchy or "degree"—the theory that everything has its proper place on a graduated scale that extends from the Creator down to the meanest object. In broad outline, Simms felt, the South already possessed a social order that proved the validity of this classic precept; there was an "aristocracy," a middle grouping, and a lower rank of slaves to support the

whole structure. But not all men—even in the South—agreed that the Negro was properly fulfilling himself by being forced to remain in subjugation. A defense of the necessity for slavery in the overall scheme of things became, therefore, one of Simms's most important tasks, both in his nonfiction and in his many romances.

A focal expression of these views—one in which Simms anatomized the problem of a structured society on its most immediate level—is to be found in his long reply to a foreign observer who had dared to attack the South in the most sensitive spot of the body politic. This English visitor-critic was Harriet Martineau, whose *Society in America* appeared in 1837, not long after Simms had entered upon his career as fiction writer. In general Miss Martineau was sympathetic toward American principles, but her assault upon the institution of slavery was specific and caustic enough to stir up vicious retort in the South. Simms's answer, first published in the Richmond *Southern Literary Messenger* in 1837 and reprinted as late as 1852,[4] is discursive and over-emotional; but it remains a valuable compendium of his basic social theory.

Simms opened his case for slavery by positing as his central principle the necessity for order in the universe. Having quoted a famous passage from Shakespeare—the speech of Ulysses on "degree" in *Troilus and Cressida*—he arrived at this key statement of his concept of a harmonious world:

Degree, or things in their proper places, is well insisted upon. All harmonies, whether in the moral or physical worlds—arise, entirely, from the inequality of the tones; and all things, in art, nature, moral and political systems, would give discord or monotony, but for this very inequality. The equality insisted upon by the levellers, would result in the necessary forfeiture of names to things, and all barriers of present distinction would be broken down. This, too, would be against the very nature of man, whose perpetual effort is to rise above his fellows. This was not in the contemplation of the fathers of our country. They were democrats, not levellers. Democracy is not levelling—it is, properly defined, the harmony of the moral world. It insists upon inequalities, as its law declares, that all men should hold the place to which they are properly entitled. The definition of true liberty is, the undisturbed possession of that place in society to which our moral and intellectual merits entitle us. *He is a free-*

*man, whatever his condition, who fills his proper place. He is
a slave only, who is forced into a position in society below the
claims of his intellect. He cannot but be a tyrant who is found
in a position for which his mind is unprepared, and to which it
is inferior* [653; the italics are Simms's].

All these are commonplace enough ideas, but they provide an
entry into the world of Simms's fiction. For as a romancer he
was to dramatize these notions in imagined actions; from aristocrat down to slave, each member of his Southern society had a
duty: "all men should hold the place to which they are properly
entitled." Recognition of and remaining in one's proper place
in this "Great Chain of Being" thus became an important plot
constituent; sometimes a character even required the aid of
others in apprehending the functions he ought to perform in
his station.

On one point only—the loose morals of some few slaveholders—
did Simms concede any ground to Miss Martineau, but this
admission carried him to his concluding and clinching argument.
Agreeing, as she had charged, that there were masters who had
misused their slaves in order to gratify vicious passions, he
observed that the real immorality involved was breach of contract
with God. For God, Simms maintained, approved the institution
of slavery as a means of rescuing and preserving the savage
from his own base inclinations. Having been taken from a
country where his only destiny was "to eat his fellow, or to be
eaten by him," the Negro now possessed recognizable advantages
from his supposedly unjust bondage: servitude increased his
fecundity, health and strength; it improved his "physical symmetry and animal organization"; it elevated his mind and morals;
it extended the term of his life; and it gave him better and more
certain food, clothing, and medical care. On the basis of such
assumed gains to the Negro, Simms then proclaimed:

These clearly establish the morality of the slave institutions in
the south;—and, though they may not prove them perfect as
they may be made, clearly maintain their propriety and the
necessity of preserving them. Indeed, the slaveholders of the
south, having the moral and animal guardianship of an ignorant
and irresponsible people under their control, are the great moral
conservators, in one powerful interest, of the entire world. There
is no propriety in the application of the name of slave to the

servile of the south. He is under no despotic power. There are laws which protect him, *in his place*, as inflexible as those which his proprietor is required to obey, *in his place*. *Providence has placed him in our hands, for his good, and has paid us from his labor for our guardianship* [657; italics Simms's].

Here we have it: a definitive statement of the argument that was to be parroted by countless Southern defenders of the system until war made further rhetorical debate futile. As they saw the issue, God was on their side so long as they acknowledged His wishes; slavery, properly understood, was a "sacred duty, undertaken to God and man alike."

Into Simms's discussion of slavery itself, with all its rationalizations and logical flaws, it is not our place to enter. What concerns us is the recognition that, as early as 1837, he had appeared as a direct spokesman for the South in one of the important periodicals of his day. From that time until an April week at Appomattox he was—in reviews, editorials, essays, and speeches— to be an indefatigable advocate of the South's right to organize society as it saw fit. It is no surprise that such an involvement in practical affairs would help to shape his fiction.

III   *The South of the Mind*

Between 1833 and 1859 Simms published more than thirty volumes of fiction. He himself classified these tales according to subject matter in letters to various correspondents[5] and also in the groupings he made for the collected edition of the 1850's; it is still helpful in tackling his large shelf to supply such a thematic breakdown.

The majority of readers have agreed that Simms's most successful work is to be found in the seven-volume series which treats of the American Revolutionary campaign in the lower South; in order of appearance these were: *The Partisan, Mellichampe, The Kinsmen* (later called *The Scout*), *Katharine Walton, The Sword and the Distaff* (revised as *Woodcraft*), *The Forayers,* and *Eutaw*. The second largest grouping is the "border" romances, or those tales set in various Southern states; usually included among these are: *Guy Rivers, Richard Hurdis, Border Beagles, Beauchampe, Charlemont,* and *Helen Halsey*. Two other books may be termed "colonial" romances: his single most popular work, *The Yemassee*, and *The Cassique of Kiawah*. Simms also attempted the "psychological" novel, in *Confession*; and (with little success) the foreign romance, in *Pelayo, Count Julian, The Damsel of Darien,* and *Vasconselos*. Further, he collected some of his shorter fiction in *The Book of My Lady, Southward Ho!* and in *The Wigwam and the Cabin*. In my estimation slightly more than a third of the total number of volumes forms the most significant body of his fiction, and it is upon these tales that I have concentrated my discussions in succeeding chapters.

Before turning to examination of these individual works, however, I consider it useful to anticipate a bit and to summarize first the overall legend of the South which finally emerged from the thousands of pages of his stories. In general, Simms based his plots upon the actual history of the South from the colonial foundations of South Carolina in the seventeenth century down to the slave-supported society of the late 1850's. But he developed this historical frame in no rigidly planned way, and—as I will demonstrate in the next chapter—he exercised the privilege of the romancer in handling his factual materials in a free, imaginative manner.

As he surveyed the South's historical and cultural growth, Simms saw the region (1) arising as a separate nation during a "heroic" period in colonial times and in the American Revolution; (2) moving through a postwar period of expansion into the border areas; and (3) emerging by the middle of the nineteenth century as a structured society with a good chance of perfecting itself into an absolutely stable order. Through the dozens of tales which he devoted to this design moves a cast which includes nearly every type of person who played any vital role in the South during three centuries—a diverse crowd unmatched in scope in the writings of any other ante-bellum Southern author. Over this welter of historical detail and this packed gallery of characters Simms exercised control through regular attention to a central organizing principle—the South as a unique social structure.

This society was, first, a real and observable one; it existed in time and space, and its components may be studied in the pages both of factual histories and of other fictional works. But in the mind of Simms himself it took on altered proportions and extended significations. It was, for him, *the* essential American society in the process of forming; it was to be the fulfillment of the dream of old Europe when it realized the possibilities of a new life in a New World. It was, as he initially conceived it, destined to lead the whole American nation up the scale of perfectibility; only when he comprehended that the North was as stubborn as the South in its concepts of society was he to argue that the South must take the way alone.

As Simms viewed it, and as he developed its pattern in his fiction, Southern society had three basic and quite distinct orders. First was the aristocratic, or leader, class; second came an assorted middle group of merchants, artisans, small farmers, frontiersmen, and others; last stood the lower orders—the Negro slaves (who were to remain fixed) and the outlaws and other misfits, who would gradually be thinned out as society perfected itself. All three groups were closely bound in a complex system of interaction; some flexibility was to be granted as an individual sought his proper place on the scale, but Simms considered the process as inclining toward an eventually stable state.

Like other theorists of an ordered society, Simms was most concerned with the leader class. In his fiction he portrayed them as the Singletons, the Waltons, the Sinclairs—old, wealthy, land-holding families whose pedigrees sometimes went back to the "baronies" of colonial South Carolina or to the nobility of Britain. By virtue of intelligence, education, and the responsibility to home and country which resulted from their control of the major portion of the land, they were suited to be the first and natural rulers in a wild and uncultivated domain. They represented tradition and continuity, and their innate sense of justice and order was to prove invaluable to the culture to which they were now devoting their own futures. Members of this native aristocracy appear regularly in Simms's fiction, and many readers are apt to condemn them as simply the counterparts of the lords and ladies of romantic fiction or to scoff at what they take to be Simms's toadying to the ruling circles of Charleston. But to adopt such an attitude is to miss what Simms actually reveals about his upper-level society. For he is highly critical of failure among its members, and he makes fundamental conflicts within the group a central theme of several of the Revolutionary tales. The right to power can be forfeited, Simms constantly reminds his readers, by a leader's refusal or inability to recognize concomitant responsibility. The world of the colonial and Revolutionary periods was not yet stabilized, and only those who continued to meet the challenge of disorder deserved to retain any hereditary rights. It may be urged that some of the younger nobles and most of the heroines are overly idealized in manners and in personal appearance, but such external portraiture was a romantic convention of fiction from which Simms could not easily free himself. Wooden his leaders often are—but they are not, the close reader will observe, wooden idols.

The second class of society, as Simms reconstructed it fictionally, was naturally the most varied. It was an amorphous group, with each member seeking his own proper place; but it also had responsibilities to the classes above and below it. It sustained and fed the aristocracy, both literally and figuratively; and on occasion it had forcibly to direct a wrongheaded young leader back to his proper path. The key figure in the performance of this latter function was the frontiersman, scout, or borderer. Symbolically, he stood for the recent native product of the forest, clearing, and swamp—just as the hero was the type formed by the settled and more stable city and plantation culture, with its European heritage. The scout often was, as Simms directly termed him, a "natural noble"; and it was he who, with more education and polishing, would be welcomed by the upper ranks of a future day.

In Simms, the scout and the young noble represent halves of a developing type—the ideal Southern leader; only their close interrelationship could bring each to the full development of his latent capabilities. This was a theme which, as we will see, he was to dramatize in several important tales. Simms's insistence upon the right of the "natural noble" to rise higher in the scale did not mean that there would not continue to be professional men, merchants, proprietors of small farms, and all the rest. But any individual among them who exhibited the requisite qualities was to be assured of the *opportunity* to ascend to a closer tie with the ruling orders.

Within the lowest class, the unalterable position of the slaves was ordained, as Simms's reply to Miss Martineau made forcefully clear. They had to continue, throughout foreseeable time, acting as the tillers and harvesters of the soil, as the cooks, the gardeners, and the house and body servants. But in his fiction, in contrast to his polemical journalistic defenses of the South's "peculiar institution," Simms ordinarily made this point obliquely by emphasizing a mutual affection between master and slave and by always asserting what he took to be the resultant benefits of the system to the Negro. As for the other dwellers on this bottom level—outlaws, squatters, Indians, poor-whites—Simms's position was just as adamant. If they could not be improved by training and led to perform socially useful functions, they would be driven out. Simms treated many of these misfits as the unfortunate but inevitable by-products of an age of transition; with the achievement of a more ordered world, they would have to spurn their behavioral pattern of sponging on society or they would face annihilation.

It must be noted, finally, that Simms throughout all his fiction portrayed Southern society as in the process of *becoming*. It had been born in colonial days and it grew up in the clashes of the Revolution; but that "heroic" time was not in itself the Golden Age, however applicable its lessons might be for the present. The Golden Age still loomed ahead; unlike some other Southern apologists, Simms did not make the claim—at least in his romances—that total perfection was already a Southern accomplishment. It is true that in the world of practical affairs he became, as war loomed, increasingly shrill and dogmatic; but in the realm of his imagination he took care to portray the disparities, the tensions, and the violence out of which order would one day evolve. It was a strange dream, and it was to prove a tragically delusive one; but whatever power the fiction of Simms still has arises entirely from his commitment to it.

IV *Simms and Southern Fiction*

At the time when Simms entered upon the principal phase of his career in the 1830's, American fiction was still in comparative adolescence. A very few authors like Charles Brockden Brown, Washington Irving, and James Fenimore Cooper had won reputations that extended even to Europe; and many lesser writers were catering to a relatively wide reading audience with tales in the sentimental, didactic, Gothic, adventure, or historical vein.

But fiction of any sort was not considered a high art either by professional critics or by ordinary readers; indeed, in many quarters there was still prejudice against it for its supposed tendency toward immorality and for its seductive appeal to the idle mind. Like Hawthorne and Poe, Simms was concerned with elevating the status of fiction; and, as I will show in detail in the next chapter, he convinced himself that it could properly have an attraction for the more serious, sophisticated literary taste.

Most of the novelists and romance writers who had a measurable influence upon Simms were Northerners or Europeans; but as a regular reviewer and as an exponent of a native Southern literature he was also in close touch with the work of his compatriots. In order to review briefly Simms's relationship to his contemporaries, we may divide prose fiction treating of the Old South into three main categories: (1) regional sketches, chiefly the work of journalistic humorists; (2) fiction dealing with Southern types or scenes, but in which the South serves merely as backdrop and in which no thoroughgoing attempt is made to differentiate Southern characters and manners; (3) fiction which has as one of its chief ends the exhibition of whatever is uniquely Southern—which strives to realize the South as a separate geographical and social unit.

Of these three categories, the work of the humorists now seems the most entertaining and distinctive to the modern reader, but it had little direct influence upon Simms. He knew Augustus Baldwin Longstreet's *Georgia Scenes* (1835), and he acknowledged it as a pioneer effort in regional writing; yet it left no visible impress upon his own fiction. Nor can any connection be seen with the productions of several other widely read creators of comic sketches: William Tappan Thompson, who contributed the figure of "Major Jones"; Johnson Jones Hooper, whose "Captain Simon Suggs" was popular in all areas; or Joseph Glover Baldwin, whose *The Flush Times of Alabama and Mississippi* (1853) is an acute portrayal of some aspects of the Southwest border country through which Simms had himself traveled. Most of these comic tales were ephemeral; they appeared chiefly in newspapers, not in the more pretentious Southern literary magazines; and, with the exception of a few like those just cited, they were not often collected in book form.

Moreover, to Simms, they were subliterary in content and style, and they did little to contribute to that elevation of Southern manners and morals for which he strove.

As early "realists" and local colorists, such writers often managed to preserve the external characteristics of the more flamboyant Southern types: the quack, the peddler, the woodsman, the confidence man, the stomp-and-gouge fighter, the hillbilly, the itinerant preacher, the stump politician. But they seldom probed below the surface, and they regularly depended for effect upon the primitive humor of the practical joke. Many of their sketches were rendered in dialect, though little care was taken in distinguishing among the varying speech patterns of the whole South; dialogue tended to be rendered as eye dialect—"uv" for "of," for example. Simms appears to have viewed frontier humor primarily as an oral art; several of his contemporaries remembered his gifts as a raconteur and his skillful imitations of regional talk. He also personally enjoyed the bawdiness and exuberance of many of the old folk tales, but he would have considered them unsuitable for a printed work which might be read by an entire family. In sum, not much typical border humor is to be found in Simms's stories. It is a fact that several of his characters are like the types celebrated in frontier tales, yet they are seldom employed for purely comic effect. The backwoodsman, for instance, that standard butt of the journalists, becomes in Simms a more idealized figure though he still speaks the traditional broad dialect. Only in some of his shorter works—in *As Good as a Comedy* (1852) or in "How Sharp Snaffles Got his Capital and Wife" (1870)—did Simms venture into the realm of broad border mirth.

Of the second type of Southern fiction—that which simply utilizes the South as a backdrop—little need be said. A number of earlier writers, including James Fenimore Cooper, had laid at least part of the action of a tale in Southern areas or had employed Southerners as characters; but they were not concerned with the South per se, and they certainly had no effect upon Simms's own concept of the region. Of prime interest, however, is the third category—those works of fiction written by Southerners in which Southern beliefs and folkways are integral. In these productions, Virginia authors originally took the lead, and at least the most important of them ought to be briefly considered.

The earliest Southern fiction writer of note to examine his area in detail was George Tucker (1775-1861). Tucker was primarily an economist, historian, biographer, and teacher (he held the chair of moral philosophy at the University of Virginia); but he is significant to literary historians for his first novel, *The Valley of Shenandoah* (1824). Tucker was unquestionably inspired by the current popularity of the Waverley novels, and he made the first attempt to do for a Southern state what Scott had done for his own region—to portray the people and customs of the recent past. Although Tucker constructed a conventional seduction plot, he recorded with some care details of the plantations, farms, and courthouses of Valley and Tidewater Virginia. Essentially, he saw the life of the period with the economist's and the historian's eye, and not with that of the creative novelist; *The Valley of Shenandoah* contributed little to the weaving of a romantic legend about "Old Virginny."[6]

Simms may not have known George Tucker's work—at least he is not mentioned in the extant letters—but he was a personal friend of another writer with the same surname, Nathaniel Beverley Tucker (1784-1851). Simms carried on a long and spirited correspondence with this prominent Virginian, who was one of the earliest and staunchest of secessionists. Beverley Tucker's main claim to literary remembrance rests on two novels published in 1836: *George Balcombe* and *The Partisan Leader*. He had spent some fifteen years in Missouri, and scenes of this border area figure largely in *George Balcombe*. Tucker tried to create vivid pictures of the frontier, but—as Simms observed—his mind was fundamentally rational and not imaginative (*L*, III, 344). Unlike George Tucker, Beverley Tucker took a complacent attitude toward slavery, and he definitely aligned himself with the sentiments of the planter class. Such views he developed further in *The Partisan Leader*, a curious work cast in the form of a prophecy of a civil war, which is belligerently propagandistic. Simms spoke of both of Tucker's fictional works with respect; but it was Tucker the ultra-Southerner who had the greatest impact upon Simms, and not his books.

With a third pioneer Southern novelist, the Baltimorean John Pendleton Kennedy (1795-1870), Simms was also personally acquainted. Each visited the other at his home, and each devoted much space in correspondence to discussion of the status of

Southern letters. But on political matters they diverged widely. Kennedy, a lawyer and sometime politician, was more allied with the merchant classes of the upper South than was any other major Southern fiction-writer of the period. As the Civil War neared, Kennedy and Simms drifted further apart in their views of the South's proper course. When the crisis came, Kennedy readily espoused the Union side, but he and Simms restored personal relations after the close of the conflict.

Kennedy made a memorable addition to Southern literature with two works: *Swallow Barn* (1832) and *Horse-Shoe Robinson* (1835). The first of these is a set of sketches of Virginia plantation life; it owes something to Irving's *Bracebridge Hall*, but it is written in a fashion that Kennedy himself felt was realistic. Simms knew this book well; and he once commented rather slyly to Kennedy that its pictures of Virginia gentlefolk were "equally true of Southern life generally" in that class and that they were "the most conclusive answers to the abolitionists, (if they *would* be answered) that could be made" (*L*, III, 122). Kennedy's second volume, *Horse-Shoe Robinson*, is a historical romance that in many ways is akin to those of Simms. A tale of the Revolution, it is partly set in South Carolina; and it was unquestionably the first to enter upon the territory which Simms was to make his own personal domain. But though both *Horse-Shoe Robinson* and Simms's *The Partisan* were published in 1835, there is no possibility of influence in either direction. Kennedy had long pondered writing this story, and Simms was discussing *The Partisan* in his correspondence before *Horse-Shoe Robinson* appeared; the similarities between the two tales can only be called a coincidence.[7] Kennedy had no long-range plan (as Simms had from the first) of treating the Revolution in a series of fictional works, and he returned to the historical romance only one more time, with *Rob of the Bowl* (1838), a narrative of colonial Maryland.

Simms—perhaps because of latent jealousy, perhaps because of their political differences—was not entirely pleased with Kennedy's work in "his" field; and when the revised edition of *Horse-Shoe Robinson* was issued in 1852 he gave it a rather carping notice. Like many other readers, Simms did find praise for the titular hero, and it is conceivable that the development of the figure of the scout in Simms's later tales owes something to Horse-Shoe's popularity. It must be observed, though, that Simms knew the character type much better than did Kennedy and also that the subject of the Revolution belonged much more to Simms through family background and wide research.

There were other Southern fiction writers—for example, William A. Caruthers (1802-46), occasionally recalled for his *The Cavaliers of Virginia*—who further explored Southern subjects and themes. But it would be beyond the scope of this study to attempt anything more than to suggest what relationship Simms had to this developing sectional literature. As I have noted, Simms was anticipated by several authors; and at least one of these men—Kennedy—produced a novel which ranks along with his best. But the "discovery" of the South must be credited largely to Simms. Within his contemporary group, only he devoted an entire career to the celebration of the region; only he saw in its history "epic" possibilities which he developed to the fullest. As the South's one enduring professional, Simms was for most readers *the* ante-bellum author. Certainly he contributed far more to the Southern literary scene than he received in return.[8]

CHAPTER 2

"My Works Are Romances"

I *The Romance and the Novel*

WHEN SIMMS RESPONDED in 1855 to E. A. Duyckinck's request for some personal comments on his craft for inclusion in the *Cyclopaedia of American Literature,* he supplied a useful key to the reading of his fiction. His letter succinctly outlines what I will demonstrate in detail in succeeding chapters— that Simms was insistent that in the main body of his work he had written a romantic prose epic of the South and that only the reader who understands this aim is qualified to assess properly his triumphs and failures. This was his credo, he told Duyckinck:

> The Yemassee, & in fact most of my works are *romances,* not novels. They involve sundry of the elements of heroic poetry. They are imaginative, passionate, metaphysical; they deal chiefly in trying situation, bold characterization, & elevating moral. They exhibit *invention* in large degree, & their progress is dramatic; the action being bold[,] salient, & with a regularly advancing convergence to the catastrophe. . . . In proportion as a man is imaginative is he *original,* and originality is the main secret of vitality. It is the creative mind only which may live in Belles Lettres Literature. When, therefore, you have searched me thoroughly in poetry, you have the key to my wards in prose fiction; for the poetical element is largely diffused in my novels— the imaginative & passionate. These display themselves in the inventive resource, the adaptableness of means to ends, the free characterization, the eager movement, the exciting action, the rapidity of progress. The standards of my novels—all of them—are either epic or dramatic—especially the latter [*L,* III, 388-89].

What Simms meant by the central terms "romance," "novel," and "epic" he had already more fully explained in the preface to one of his earliest works, *The Yemassee* (1835). The novel, he had observed, citing Henry Fielding and Samuel Richardson as typical authors, is "confined to the felicitous narration of common and daily occurring events"; the romance, on the other hand, "does not insist upon what is known, or even what is probable. It grasps at the possible; and, placing a human agent in hitherto untried situations, it exercises its ingenuity in extricating him from them, while describing his feelings and his fortunes in their progress."[1]

This assertion of an essential distinction between the romance and the novel was not original with Simms, nor was he always careful—as the very remarks to Duyckinck illustrate—to keep strictly to this terminology.[2] Both terms are elusive ones at best, and it is difficult to develop a single definition of romance that will describe works so diverse in form, style, and theme as *The Deerslayer*, *Mardi*, and *The House of the Seven Gables*. But it is at least possible to see why a number of American writers in the first half of the nineteenth century felt it necessary to comment on the mode of fiction which they had chosen. The domestic novel, or novel of manners—as it was practiced by Fielding, Richardson, and Jane Austen—was concerned with mirroring the everyday life of a commonplace, established social group; on the whole, it devoted itself to the interests of a middle class.

But America had as yet few urban centers, and its society was still fluid; the American writer recognized that instead of stability there was a general condition of flux, of diversity, of striving toward vaguely realized goals. The fiction in which these insights were embodied took, therefore, a more open, exciting, and imaginative form—one that often tended toward symbolic or allegorical expression. In the truest sense the romance was a "primitive" form; it had links with a medieval prototype and, even beyond that, with the ancient folktale. It employed "archetypal" situations: the testing of the hero, the journey, the disguise, the captivity, the hair-raising escape. The romance writer was not anxious, as was the novelist, about the problem of verisimilitude, of surface "reality." He regularly depended upon coincidence to resolve his plot complications, and he created dialogue that was entirely artificial in its prolixity and its rhetorical flourishes.

Perhaps American readers, confronted with the immensity and with the potentialities of the nation their ancestors had created, discerned a link between the new American hero of forest and plain and the hero of traditional European legend. Simms, at least, argued for such a connection in his further comment in the *Yemassee* Preface that "The modern romance is a poem in every sense of the word." Even more, it is "the substitute which the people of to-day offer for the ancient epic." By making this association between epic and romance Simms patently did not mean that the writer was bound by the classic rules of structure but rather that he might with "epic" sweep re-create the early history of a people and place, with emphasis upon heroic deeds and forceful characters, as an exemplar for the present day. Simms's technique of reasoning was clever, for it allowed him to answer critics of modern fiction obliquely by claiming the prose romance as a simple *extension* of ancient poetry and drama. It was the genre that had been evolved for expressing the conditions of the prosy present, but its aspirations were still "very much those of the epic."

This is a concept which many latter-day readers, conditioned by the "realistic" novel of the late nineteenth and twentieth centuries and by the "art-novel" as practiced by Henry James and Joseph Conrad, find impossible to accept seriously. And by the standards of recent fiction, the romance unquestionably is crude. It was unprogressive in its constant repetition of stock formulas, and it made small demands upon the sophisticated intellect. Obviously, too, it often was simply a wish-fulfillment fantasy; it forced its heroes and heroines into fascinating and frightening fixes, but it always contained the buried reassurance that by the final page the enemy would be vanquished, the safe haven reached, the lovers forever united. On its general popular level, it catered to the American's optimistic trust that there was no obstacle—harsh nature, wild beast, Indian, or antagonist of any category—that could not be overcome by stout heart and strong limbs. It employed the age-old symbols of light and darkness to typify the conflict of man and nature, the struggle between good and evil, the tension of man's dual nature; but on the whole it attested that the light would prevail.[3]

All of the weaknesses of the popular romance as a genre are manifest in Simms's books—but so are its strengths. He was incurably careless in overall structure and in diction, and he worked to irritating excess the nick-of-time appearance of the rescuing agent. But he often managed his suspense with effect that can still be felt; and he did adapt old literary conventions to the special conditions of Southern life. Most importantly, clinging to his concept of the romance as the "modern epic," he did develop a unique controlling theme: the rise of the South through harsh trials to status as a new nation. If, because of his need to win a wide readership, he never entirely freed himself from formulas which had succeeded so many times before, he nonetheless perceived in the romance the possibility of seriously rendering the tensions and aspirations of American life.

II *Models for Fiction*

As his prefaces and his reviews disclose, Simms was quite conscious that he was indebted to the work of a number of predecessors and contemporaries. Most obviously, he was a follower of Sir Walter Scott and of Scott's American disciple, James Fenimore Cooper. But he was an omnivorous and a retentive reader, and his romances also owe much to the Gothic novel, to William Godwin, to German romanticism, to the novel of crime of Edward Bulwer, and to his favorite Elizabethan and Jacobean playwrights.[4] If he did manage to develop an original theme, he was rarely inventive in the forms of fiction; he was an adapter rather than a breaker of new ground.

Fundamentally, what both Scott and Cooper provided for Simms was a stimulus to composition and a ready-made method of narration. Cooper had seen in Scott's handling of history in the Waverley romances a technique for the utilization of American materials, and he had promptly begun fulfilling the dreams of literary nationalists. And in Cooper's successful celebration of the American past Simms perceived a way to accomplish his own "epic" re-creation of Southern annals. For this insight Simms paid Cooper gracious tribute in a long essay on his rival's work; Cooper had, he conceded, first "wakened us to this self-reference—to this consciousness of mental resources."[5] Cooper, that is, had demonstrated that American history was not as barren of usable events as some critics had supposed; like Charles Brockden Brown and Washington Irving before him—

but far more systematically and successfully—he had made Americans more aware of their roots in the continent and of the continuity of human experience. He had, in addition, freed the Scott-type of romance from dependence on the mere facts of history—though he was to be criticized occasionally for his free handling of detail.

From both Scott and Cooper, Simms drew a number of specific plot devices: the central love story, the flight-and-pursuit motif, the use of disguise, the hand-to-hand conflict, the storming of a fortress, and many others. Further, in his "crime novels" (like the early *Martin Faber* and the later *Confession*) he also relied upon the Gothicizers and upon Godwin and Bulwer for instruction in the literary probing of secret guilt. Such elements of strong indebtedness appear to give the lie to his boast to Duyckinck of "originality"; but to Simms that term meant, in practice at least, the total effect of a work and not its plot components. He was always willing to give readers the kind of episodes he believed they wanted, and he rarely failed popular expectation. His own fiction, in short, seldom rose to his announced critical standard; only his Southern settings, the manner in which he reworked stock figures, and—especially—his controlling theme of a nation's rise, absolved him from the charge of slavish imitation.

Commentators upon Simms regularly have argued that he was unsure in his conception of character—that he was torn between a "romantic" and a "realistic" view of human nature. His noble heroes and heroines, that is to say, are usually viewed by such critics as bookish and unconvincing, while his "low" characters—his outlaw bands, for example—are praised as more "realistic" portraits taken from actual life. The judgment sounds plausible, but it is commonly made by those who have read Trent and Parrington and not much of Simms. The question ought to be raised anew: *are* the low-life characters "realistic" in any but the most superficial sense of the term? In almost every instance, so I hope to show, these rogues betray far more relationship to the traditional Gothic villain than to the poor-whites or criminals of the South Simms knew. I would ask further: *are* Simm's heroes and heroines no more than the pasteboard cut-outs of popular fiction? I contend that they appear flat and unbelievable only if the reader remains unaware that young men and women in the

Old South did strike formal attitudes, did indulge in a code of ornate manners, and did converse now and then in flights of remarkable rhetorical fancy.

It is not my intention to assert that the usual critical attitude toward Simms ought simply to be reversed. I mean only to indicate my belief that he was not striving for the "romantic" in one character type and the "realistic" in another. What most influenced his imaging of an individual—the specifics of appearance, dress, speech, and action—was quite another consideration: it was the station which that character had publicly to assume within the framework of Southern society. Put another way, Simms's standard was that of decorum; each figure had to be presented according to his or her "quality." The heroine could never be seen in her nightgown or the hero too deep in his cups; the low person, on the other hand, could be surprised in acts that would be shameful in the higher classes. Every member of the cast had necessarily to appear and to act in the way in which society at large generally observed him.

This concept of decorum Simms partly learned from his study of the Elizabethan and Jacobean drama. As he maintained in his letter to Duyckinck, both "epic" and "dramatic" were central terms for the true comprehension of his purposes. Though he usually assumed the viewpoint of omniscient author (and sometimes broke in with asides to the reader), he often did allow a character to give his own expression to inner feelings in a soliloquy. The technique was not uncommon in fiction, but Simms linked it to his general theory that the reader ought to observe a fictional personage as he would an actor upon the stage. This notion applied, significantly, to all social levels; his "realistic" figures are as prone to soliloquizing as are their "romantic" associates.

The general influence of the drama further helps to explain Simms's use of the "humour" character, the rapid shifting of scene, the alternation of incidents, and the extended passages of dialogue. As in the stage productions which his acquaintance Edwin Forrest had made such a success, swift movement and overblown rhetoric were proven devices for holding an audience's attention. Nor should it be overlooked that the dramatic method was a highly appropriate one for rendering Simms's legend of the South: in his society most of the characters are extroverted actors in a public drama; the theme of introverted isolation, which so attracted Hawthorne, was not within Simms's interest or his powers. As an actual playwright Simms was a wretched failure. His true forte was always fiction, but his enthusiasm for the theater provided him with techniques as useful as those which he had learned from his masters in the prose romance.

III *Simms on Style*

For most modern readers the greatest obstacle to appreciation of Simms is his prose style. As the enormous mass of his work attests, he composed hastily, revised rarely, and relied for effect upon exciting incident rather than upon "fine writing." Like other authors of the period, he preferred an "open" and expanded method of narration to concision or tightness of plot; and he often padded out his pages with nature description, historical summations, and tedious details of dress and personal appearance. As he admitted, his thoughts flowed faster than his pen could move; as a result, his longer sentences occasionally collapse into near-incoherence. These are undeniably primary flaws; they were condemned by some of his contemporary critics, and present-day students cannot ignore them. It is relevant to observe, however, how Simms himself answered such criticism.

Simms's close friend James Lawson once made the surprising blunder of caustically reviewing one of Simms's foreign romances, *The Damsel of Darien,* in a prominent New York journal. The book was quite as bad as Lawson said it was; knowing Simms intimately, he was well aware where at least some of the fault lay. "Mr. Simms," Lawson pointed out, "writes so much, and publishes so often, that it is next to impossible, with all his genius, that he can always avoid incorrectness of phrase, and tautology in expression."[6] Simms revenged himself on Lawson in a blistering letter that is an embarrassing mixture of wounded pride, assumed bafflement that a supposed friend could do him such an ill turn, and bad-tempered overstatement of his case. But the review at least drew out of Simms one of his most dogmatic statements about the act of composing the romance. His defense is overwrought and his reply to some of Lawson's specific points is highly labored special pleading, but on the topic of his stylistic defects he sounds entirely honest:

Mere verbal correctness, good similes, and the simple exclusion of irrelevant matter do not constitute the only, or even the greater & more distinctive essentials of a novel or romance. Is nothing to be said of the invention which it displays, the fancy, the imagination—the creative faculty which makes the material to live, breathe, & burn[?] Is nothing to be said of that epic singleness of object which, in the Damsel, fixes the eye of the Hero & the reader, equally upon one great aim & purpose which is steadily pursued, amidst trials, & tortures, & persecution, to its triumphant close[?] Is nothing to be said of the felicity of moral, & natural painting in the description of scenes equally wild, wondrous & true—scenes of strife & repose—of passion & of tenderness—of hope, fear, shame, malignity, and every passion to which man & his nature are liable[?] [L, I, 154-55].

To Simms these alone were "the larger topics which should have been discussed in the examination of the work"; since Lawson had concentrated instead upon mere "faults," the review was "unjust." The modern reader of the *Damsel* probably would side with Lawson, and it is unfortunate that Simms chose one of his weakest books for such a spirited defense. Yet some of his points are nonetheless valid; in his Revolutionary romances and in a few of the border tales he did manage, in spite of frequent verbal slackness, to keep to an "epic singleness of object," to "one great aim and purpose."

In my survey of Simms's literary career in the chapters which follow I have attempted, therefore, to concentrate on what I have found to be most viable and to avoid extended belaboring of stylistic weaknesses apparent to any reader. The "epic" nature of Simms's legend of the South is, I believe, still salvageable from the body of his romances. Occasionally, in assessing literary works, it is possible to assert that a whole of this sort can be greater than the sum of its parts.

CHAPTER 3

The Lonely Traveler

I *Apprentice Days*

SIMMS'S LITERARY CAREER from the publication of his first volume of poetry in 1825 to the appearance of his earliest works of fiction in 1833 is a calendar of frustrations and partial successes. An often moody and solitary youth, he found in Byron and other Romantic poets congenial models for his own lines; but the six volumes of puerile verse which he patched together in these years exhibit no signs of a talent which would lift him to the level of his masters.[1] These books had a fairly wide success among reviewers and readers, a reception which helped to suggest to him that he might earn a living by his pen; but otherwise they have no significance, and it is unnecessary to disinter them.

These eight apprentice years gave Simms a harsh initiation into what it meant to endeavor to be a professional writer in the ante-bellum South. After trying his hand at the law, he had been a magazine and a newspaper editor; in both professions he had smarted under financial and political reverses. During the period of his editorship, moreover, his father, grandmother, and wife had all died, leaving him with an infant daughter to support. And so, in the summer of 1832, he sold his failing newspaper (which had opposed the locally popular doctrine of Nullification) and set off for the first time for the North—without, he later recalled, "any definite idea of what I was to do for the future" (*L*, I, 165).

He was not entirely without resources, however, since he had often reviewed the productions of Northern writers and had even corresponded with some of them. With one in particular, James Lawson, a young Scot of modest literary abilities, he had already formed a friendship that was to last for the remainder of his life. The amiable Lawson at once welcomed him to New York, and largely through his kindness Simms was brought to the notice of other writers and publishers—men like William Cullen Bryant, James Kirke Paulding, Fitz-Greene Halleck, and the Harper brothers. In such an atmosphere the world of letters took on more of the gracious aspect for which he had longed; for almost the first time in his life Simms thoroughly enjoyed himself. He had carried with him the manuscript of *Atalantis,* his most ambitious poetic effort to date; and, in between literary gatherings and mild flirtations, he spent the remainder of the summer in preparing the work for the press.

By the time that this poem—a pallid Byronic and Shelleyan "story of the sea"—was issued, Simms had already determined for the present to re-establish himself in South Carolina. But his compatriots were again embroiled in one of the State's interminable political wrangles; and once more, so he wrote Lawson, he considered leaving his home forever and joining his father's brother in operating the plantation in Mississippi. But, characteristically, he added to Lawson that he had sent their friends, the Harpers, the first volume of a new novel (*Guy Rivers*) and was waiting for their reaction (*L,* I, 49). Apparently only encouragement of his experiments in fiction was required to make him change his mind about emigrating westward, and he received it. During part of 1833 he was back in New York to supervise the first book publication of one of his tales, *Martin Faber; the Story of a Criminal.*[2]

This trial novel—really little more than an expanded short story—has no intrinsic merit; but it is worth brief attention since its strained Gothic elements were soon to be resurrected in *Guy Rivers* and since Simms never rid himself entirely of a fondness for some of the worst excesses of the school of terror. The story, in the confession mode, is narrated in the first person by Martin, who is in prison under sentence of death for murdering a girl he had seduced. Martin sententiously informs the reader that, though he had come of a good family and had every advantage, an inner power with which he could not contend had brought him to his own destruction. Then in flashbacks he tells this dreary tale: Having been severely punished by his schoolmaster for malicious acts, he had arranged to have the master and his family driven from the village. Some years later, while on a hunting trip, he came upon a girl named Emily and learned that she was the daughter of his old antagonist. Furthering his revenge, he seduced Emily, and for a time carried on an affair with her. But soon he became engaged to the "young, beautiful and wealthy" Constance Claiborne and decided that he and Emily had to part. Emily pleaded that she was pregnant and threatened to go to Constance; Martin, now fed up with her, strangled her and hid her body in the cavity of a large rock.

Martin married Constance, but Emily was not to be stilled: her ghost appeared to mock him at the ceremony and on his wedding night. As if this visitation were not enough to fret about, Martin began to suspect an intimacy between his wife and an old school friend, William Harding; to try to force the truth out, he did everything possible to throw them together. But the astute Harding, sensing that Martin had a motive behind this bizarre behavior, undertook a little detective work and, with oddly little trouble, soon uncovered Martin's crime. In a flamboyant denouement, Harding accused Martin at the scene of the murder and had the rock blasted open before a crowd of villagers, thereby revealing Emily, who was still clutching a cameo of Martin's. Seized and taken to prison, Martin vainly attempted to stab himself and Constance. As the tale concludes, he is led off to execution while crying out: "O cursed weakness, that I should fail at that moment of escape—" (188).

This foolish story is patently a mélange of Gothic and sentimental plot clichés, and it would be pointless to seek its source in William Godwin's *Caleb Williams* or in any other single work. The mark of Godwin is indeed upon it—but so is that of Bulwer, Schiller, and a host of the more popular German, English, and American Gothic tale-tellers. It is a measure of the taste of the era that so poorly constructed and narrated a tale could find an audience; but it was enthusiastically bought, and Simms was heartened enough to bring out late in the same year *The Book of My Lady*, a gathering of the milk-and-water sketches, stories, and poems which had appeared in various periodicals.

With these two volumes of fiction the apprentice phase of Simms's career was closed. He had now established himself as a professional writer; he had made himself known in New York as well as in Charleston; and he was convinced of his powers—almost arrogantly so. Yet it is clear that what was most wanting in his work to date was an original subject to which he could devote all his undeniable energy and talent. He was presumably not conscious that it would become a lifelong commitment, but he was to begin to explore a basically new idea in his succeeding volumes. This theme was, of course, his own South.

Simms had not yet been entirely contented in the South nor, despite his political interests, had he wholeheartedly given himself to it. But his experience of many levels of Southern society was already an integral part of him; it needed only to be recognized as material to be turned to fictional use. He had known old Charleston, plantation life, and the raw frontier; and he had once dreamed that he might be able to celebrate the region as an epic poet would. To attempt to bring all three areas—town, plantation, and border—into a meaningful relationship was to be the task of his fiction from this point on; the strategy he developed was to treat them as the components of an achievable ideal society. It was a myth that was long and involved in the making, but he was to start confidently to undertake it in his next three books—*Guy Rivers, The Yemassee,* and *The Partisan.*

II *A Tale of Georgia*

Not long before the publication of his first full-length romance, *Guy Rivers* (1834), Simms wrote to Lawson to clear up a misunderstanding: The new book was not about political quarrels in South Carolina, as one paper had announced. Instead, it was "a tale of Georgia—a tale of the miners—of a frontier and wild people, and the events are precisely such as may occur among a people & in a region of that character" (*L,* I, 55). As Simms's letter intimates, he was convinced that the setting and the actors were new to American fiction. Although A. B. Longstreet was publishing his "Georgia Scenes" in newspaper installments, Simms was then unaware of these sketches; and he felt that the topic of the local frontier was his alone.

Certainly he was now sufficiently prepared to be a pioneer in Southern fiction. In his trips across the lower states, often on horseback through wilderness and recently settled border areas, he had stored his mind with images of these "wild people"—of outlaw bands, of frontiersmen, of adventurers and outcasts from the settled East, of Indian tribes gradually being driven westward from their old grounds, of squatters in hovels, of small villages with only a thin veneer of law and order. From memories of some of these experiences Simms had already drawn for his volumes of poetry and for the sketches collected in *The Book of My Lady*. But such use of materials had been almost casual; it was simply one element of the exoticism he was purveying to genteel readers. In *Guy Rivers,* suddenly and for the first time, he made a bold attempt to communicate a fuller view of the Southern frontier, to render the specific scene as well as general atmosphere.

What had led Simms at this time to turn to his own adventures for a subject? The immediate spur was the favorable reception of his first two prose works and the implied promise that he could succeed as a professional writer. There were dollars and distinction yet to be won—but how? As he recognized, the content of his early stories was distressingly thin, the characters weakly drawn, the locales (particularly in *Martin Faber*) vaguely realized. He needed to expand his horizons to fulfill his threefold ambition: to make money, to raise the prestige of fiction, and to do service to his region. The examples of Scott and Cooper showed the way. Both had contrived to give a romantic and even "epic" lift to local scenes; both had been spectacularly popular. It was at least possible, Simms saw, that their formula could be made to work again by turning it to the little-known territory through which he had traveled—especially the Georgia gold area, which was then exciting high public interest.

However, another strong literary influence kept Simms from any slavish imitation of Scott and Cooper, from simply transferring a love-and-adventure tale to the South. This was his attraction to the novel of purpose—especially to studies of crime like Edward Bulwer's *Paul Clifford* (1830) and *Eugene Aram* (1832). *Martin Faber* had already exposed this interest; in it Simms had argued that only a moral intention—an analysis of character to illuminate either worth or wickedness—could lift a work of fiction to the status of a significant art form. Unfortunately, his talents were not compatible with such a forthright didactic purpose. Deep psychological probing was never his forte; the complication and unraveling of a thrilling tale was. This basic conflict of intention marred a number of his books; in an especially clear-cut form it may be studied in *Guy Rivers*. This "tale of Georgia," then, can best be examined by separate consideration of its two main plot lines—the first treating of the outlaw Guy Rivers, the second devoted to the proper young hero, Ralph Colleton.

Obvious similarities between the natures of Guy Rivers and Martin Faber suggest that what Simms had originally contemplated as the subject of *Guy Rivers*—perhaps *before* the frontier setting was hit upon—was another commonplace Gothic tale in which terror and vice could be fully exploited for the reader's delight—and then justified by a moralizing dissection of the villain's makeup. This must have been Simms's initial intention, for he advises us in his preface that he has endeavored to "glance somewhat into causes" as a "physician of the human mind."[3] He does venture to account partially for Guy's depraved actions by informing us that his mother laxly permitted him to have his own way. But this "glance into causes" is no more than that; Guy's theatrical trappings make us forget that he has a mind at all.

Guy Rivers is a brigand, the leader of a band which roams the Georgia gold fields preying upon travelers and performing other wickedness. Once a brilliant lawyer, he was thwarted both in ambition and in love; these frustrations, Simms adds, helped drive him to a career of crime. But despite all of Simms's tedious efforts to turn him into a living figure of the untamed frontier, Guy remains a literary paste-up: he is the Elizabethan revenger of the tragedy of blood, the villain-hero of Bulwer, and Byron's Cain. Successful outlaw though he is, Guy is a trial to his cohorts. Not willing just to take the booty and let the bloodshed go, he has to plot, posture, and rant, even before his own gang. "You are too fierce and furious," one of his lieutenants warns him, when Guy learns that a young stranger, Ralph Colleton, is the person who had wounded him during a holdup attempt—and also the lad to whom he had lost the girl he wanted. "What do you think to do, Guy, . . ." his comrade asks; "what would satisfy you?" "His blood—his blood!" Guy passionately cries. This gratuitous brutality is too much for the underling, who starts back with "undisguised horror" and shudders at "the fiendlike look that met his own" (131).

This is precisely the trouble: Guy *is* a fiend and no amount of rhetoric on his or Simms's part can convince us that he has a counterpart on the border or anywhere else. His plots against Ralph and his own eventual capture by the law in his castle-like hideout are straight melodrama; and his mutters of self-justification—Simms's attempt to shore up his character—carry no conviction that a human being is speaking. Even his suicide in jail, with his castoff mistress beside him, creates none of the pathos and regret for a wasted life for which Simms strove. Nothing but red ink flows from his fatal wound.

With his young hero, Ralph Colleton, Simms manages to be somewhat more original. He is Simms's first portrait of a young Southern aristocrat, the prototype of a long line; as such he is fittingly introduced in the tradition of high romance. As the book opens, Ralph, a lonely traveler on horseback, rides at sunset across the barren hills of Georgia and right into a nest of villainy; but we are soon made to understand that he is something more than the romancer's dream man—despite his waves of dark hair, his high and intellectual forehead, and his commanding bearing. For Ralph, Simms is quick to inform us, is a South Carolinian of good family and a prime specimen from an area "famous for its wealth, lofty pride, polished manners, and noble and considerate hospitality" (36). Unhappily, it is this "lofty pride" that has driven Ralph into the wild frontier. Blocked by his uncle from marriage with his cousin Edith, he has stalked out of the house and resolved to return to Tennessee, where he had been brought up by his now-deceased father. Pride, we discover, has also been the motive of his uncle in opposing the union, but his haughtiness is not to be condoned because it stems from material snobbery. As Simms editorializes, the uncle "had learned to value wealth as a substitute for mind—for morals—for all that is lofty . . ." (37). On the other hand, Ralph's father, quite a different sort, had married beneath his social station; his wife brought him no dowry and he had exiled himself from Carolina society after he outlived his own fortune.

Because of his overriding concern with the Guy Rivers plot

line, Simms does not fully develop this matter of family pride (and its associations with an established social order), but he does at least suggest its significance. Ralph, the young hot-head, must face the violent tests of the frontier (including a false accusation of murder and a trial by local standards of justice) before he can understand that he has acted hastily and for unworthy reasons. As a potential Southern leader, he must see all levels of society in operation and thus come to know himself and his place on the scale. After he is cleared of the charge (a plot of Guy Rivers, naturally), he is reconciled with his now chastened uncle and returns with him and Edith to take up his proper role on the plantation.

One more character gives us a foretaste of a second Southern type that Simms was to consider at length in other tales. He is Mark Forrester, a borderer who befriends Ralph while Guy plots against him and who becomes his "squire." Mark is a "natural noble," the independent and unsophisticated man of the open air who functions to deflate the hero's pomposity and to bring him to a clearer sense of his real duties. In Simms's later treatment of this character type—for example, Jack Bannister in *The Scout*—the frontiersman was to be accepted as an integral part of the structure of Southern society. But here Mark is a minor actor, and Simms kills him off early in order to hurry back to Guy's stronghold.

The "extras" in the cast are what we might anticipate in an early work; some are directly derived from Simms's reading and a few others come at least partly from his personal observation of the backwoods. A Yankee peddler with his worthless wares is simply the shrewd trader of American folk tales; if Simms had seen such a man on his travels, he made less use of his eyes than of tradition in drawing the New Englander. A glimpse of a field preacher is more successful; Simms obviously delighted in the colloquial language that could reach the untutored minds of the borderers. And several other minor characters—the squatters in the gold fields, the Georgia guardsmen, a family of pioneers heading West in a wagon—are carefully delineated though their relevance to the main plot is of little importance.

The two principal female characters—Edith, Ralph's destined bride, and Lucy Munro, a border girl who also falls for him—are straight out of the waxworks. Hopelessly virtuous, conventionally sentimental, they oppress the reader with their bursts of high-falutin talk, which Simms ruthlessly imitated from the dialogue of a string of romantic heroines. After one especially soggy passage between Ralph and Lucy, Mark Forrester appears to give the game away by commenting to Ralph: "Doesn't she talk like a book?" (149)—but naïve Mark, of course, is paying a compliment. No American author of this period created believable women, and we would hardly expect Simms to succeed where his superiors failed. Yet he may have had more reason than they behind his pallid portraiture. By placing the Lady on a pedestal, the Southerner made her appear vapid and remote; but he also kept her from thinking about the rights of women—and of Negroes. Since he encouraged her display of a "finer nature," he ran the danger of her turning social critic. Attempting to channel her emotional drive into sentimentality was one way of forestalling the threat. Simms possibly felt that putting her into a book also gave her a text to copy.

Considered as a whole, *Guy Rivers* fails because it tries unsuccessfully to join two disparate plot lines: Guy and Ralph Colleton simply cannot inhabit the same literary world. And yet writing it was a valuable experience for Simms; it gave him the opportunity to test his techniques of narration on a broad scale. He was also learning more about the handling of suspense, of the importance of minor characters, and the use of setting in the creation of internal plausibility. His word sense was still faulty (he improved the style considerably in the 1855 revision), and his concept of structure was unsure. But he had found his central subject of the South, and he had at least sketched the young aristocrat and the frontiersman. For Simms himself, the practice gained from *Guy Rivers* outweighed its weaknesses.

III *The Last of the Yemassees*

Among the readers of its day *Guy Rivers* was a resounding hit. Praise from Southerners might have been anticipated, but the often vicious New York press was surprisingly favorable, with many reviewers acclaiming the birth of an important new talent. Inevitably the book stimulated comparisons with Cooper's tales, often to the detriment of the "American Scott." "We would set it above every American novel that has met our eye," pronounced the editor of the *American Monthly Magazine.* "Cooper, great as he is in graphic detail, could not have written Guy Rivers had he died for it." And the New York *American* declared: "There has been no American novel since the days when the appearance of Mr. Cooper's *Spy* created such a sensation in our reading public, that has excited half the interest that will attend the circulation of *Guy Rivers.*"[4] Most significantly for Simms's future career, several commentators made special mention of the Southern frontier setting and predicted that the "untrodden paths" he had set out upon would be more fully explored.

To the frontier Simms did again return in his next romance, *The Yemassee* (1835), but the friendly reception of *Guy Rivers* was not the immediate stimulus for his choice of locale. For, as a letter written about the time *Guy Rivers* appeared makes clear, he had already been "digesting the plan of an Indian Tale—a story of an early settlement and of an old tribe in Carolina" (*L*, I, 61). Unfortunately, the extant later letters throw little light upon the genesis of this "Indian tale," but as a literary topic the aboriginals had long fascinated him. Indian legends had been the subject of several of the sketches in *The Book of My Lady;* and an early poem, "The Last of the Yemassees," printed in his 1827 collection, had dealt with the same period and area he was now mulling over for a new romance. His initial interest, then, in the frontier region—probably stemming from the tales he had heard from his grandmother—had been centered on the time when the Indians and the colonists lived in close contact. Thus *The Yemassee* might have appeared before *Guy Rivers* had it not been for Simms's evident desire to capitalize on the widespread curiosity about the Georgia gold diggings.

Composing with characteristic rapidity, Simms had *The Yemassee* ready within the year after *Guy Rivers* reached its public. "A Romance of Carolina" he subtitled the new book, and in its brief but important preface (discussed in Chapter II) he tried to explain his distinction between the novel and the romance. There is a notable sense of assurance in this foreword, a self-confidence that sprang from something deeper than the pride of a young author who had been kindly treated by his critics. For Simms knew that he had found his proper subject; he saw that the possibilities for future treatment were limitless. He was on home ground now, and in this tale of colonial warfare he made his first positive statement of the meaning of his region's past.

The subject of *The Yemassee* is the uprising in 1715 of the Yemassee Indians against the British colonists of South Carolina— an actual historical event which Simms saw as significant because it represented the overcoming of the second of the great obstacles that his budding Southern nation faced. The first had been the forbidding wilderness itself; the next, the aboriginals, he disposed of in this romance; the third barrier—that of a mother country bent on keeping its colonies in permanent subjugation—became the theme of his next work, *The Partisan,* and of the succeeding Revolutionary romances.

By the first quarter of the eighteenth century, the date of *The Yemassee's* action, the Carolinians had already made advances into the fertile, primeval land; but the Indians were becoming stubborn about continued encroachment upon their ancient tribal preserve. *The Yemassee* thus falls naturally into two parallel plot lines: the struggle told from the viewpoint of the Indians and from that of the settlers who are anticipating an outbreak. This dual focus allowed Simms two major actors: Sanutee, the Yemassee chief once helpful to the colonists; and Governor Charles Craven, who disguises himself as "Gabriel Harrison" in order to prowl about the countryside and assess the coming threat.

Much has been written about the accuracy of Simms's portrait of the Indian and about his retelling of the Yemassee War.[5] But it would be an error to suppose that his main interest was in authenticity, despite his quick summation of the end of the conflict in his final chapter and his flaunting of historical sources in his footnotes. For the book's major theme is what the colonists and the Indians signify in terms of a growing civilization in the South, and he exercises fully the romancer's privilege (which he argues for in his preface) to weave the facts of history into a wholly fictional main plot.

With Simms's own aim in mind, we may observe that the Indians are first made to represent a direct tie with an ancient past. Like most Americans of his day, Simms had been irritated by the sneers of foreign visitors at the nation's youth and cultural rawness. He perceived that in the Indians, however, the country did have a living link with a remote age. He enlarges this notion in *The Yemassee* by frequent attention to details of tribal structure, to the Indians' mythology (which, he confesses in his 1853 preface, he entirely invented!), and to hallowed customs and rituals. He even suggests a link between the Indians and the early inhabitants of the Old World:

> The elements of all uncultivated people are the same. The early Greeks, in their stern endurance of torment, in their sports and exercises, were exceedingly like the North American savages. The Lacedaemonians went to battle with songs and dances; a similar practice obtained among the Jews; and one particularly, alike of the Danes and Saxons, was to usher in the combat with wild and discordant anthems.[6]

It was to a land already long the abode of men that the English settlers came, but the encounter between the Old World and the New was to result in a changed order for both. The import of this clash of cultures has been brought home to Sanutee, the chieftain who had welcomed the newcomers but who now plans to lead his people in a war to exterminate the whites. The altered condition of his society is symbolized in the degradation of his own son, Occonestoga, whose body and will have been sapped by the settlers' liquor. Because Occonestoga appears incapable of regeneration, Sanutee has disowned him and has ordered the most dreaded of dooms pronounced upon him: he is to be expelled from the tribe and to have his tribal tattoo cut from his flesh. But later in the tale, as this ceremony is being described, Sanutee's wife, Matiwan, rushes in and preserves her son from disgrace and damnation by fatally tomahawking the corrupted youth. Sanutee's own death in the final battle therefore means the end of the Yemassee dynasty.

For the stoic courage which Sanutee and Matiwan show, Simms allows human sympathy; but he does not permit us to be carried away into approval of the Indian cause. Though the natives have had a prior claim to the land, their reign as "the nation" is necessarily finished; unlike the Negroes, they cannot even be absorbed into the white society. In a long argument over the Indian question between Hugh Grayson, a young colonist, and the Rev. Mr. Matthews, the settlement's pastor, Simms's own point of view is clearly that expressed by Grayson:

"[I]t is utterly impossible that the whites and Indians should ever live together and agree. The nature of things is against it, and the very difference between the two, that of colour, perceptible to our most ready sentinel, the sight, must always constitute them an inferior caste in our minds . . ." (325).

Having introduced this doctrine of white supremacy, Grayson goes on to argue that, with the colonists' advance, the Indians will lose more and more of their hunting grounds; and, if they are allowed to skulk about, they will sink further into poverty and degeneracy. The solution Grayson offers is an extreme one: "[T]o my mind, the best thing we can do for them is to send them as far as possible from communion with our people" (326).

How this removal was to be accomplished Simms does not explain, and it is a drastic proposal to come from one who had occasionally celebrated the "noble savage" in early poems and tales. But Simms could imagine no place for the Indians in a civilized society, and he refused—at least in his fiction—to give much further attention to them. The white man could learn woodcraft from the Indians, and historically they had served as a reminder of the antiquity of the American land. But they could not be turned into slaves, and their basic natures were too brutal to allow any other integration into society. Hence they had to be driven westward to work out their own fates.[7]

Because the Indian problem is in the process of being resolved in *The Yemassee*, Simms does not here suggest more than a broad outline of the colony's social structure. But there are, nonetheless, representatives of each part of his threefold system: leader, middle class, and lower order. Gentry comes into the book in the person of an actual Englishman of rank, Governor Craven—or Gabriel Harrison, as he prefers to be known during most of the story's action. Probably because he is based on a real figure of the early colony, Harrison—who springs from an old Cavalier family—is more lighthearted in manner than are most of Simms's other representatives of the leader class. But that he *is* the leader, charged with the preservation of his people in a time of peril, is never in question. As he moves on his secret mission among the Indians and border settlers, Harrison carries with him the destiny of a rising nation.

Harrison's character is straightforward and needs little explication. More interestingly, Simms also gives some attention to another type of potential leader who was to become increasingly prominent in his later fiction—the youth who, though qualified by innate worth and intelligence to assume high rank, needs to be purged of headstrongness through extreme trials. In *The Yemassee* such a man is Hugh Grayson, who during most of the action strikes the reader as a boor and a bore because of his moroseness, his flashes of hot temper, his attack upon Harrison, and particularly because of his hopeless efforts to win Bess Matthews (the beloved of Harrison). But by the close of the tale Hugh has been through the purifying fire; and, brought to self-knowledge by the rebukes of Bess and by his discovery during the Indian fighting of his faculty of leadership, he emerges in a new aspect. Because of this somewhat puzzling reversal in a man we had thought to be a sniveling bully, Simms steps into the story with this direct comment:

> [W]ith all his faults, and they were many, [Hugh] was in reality a noble fellow. Full of a high ambition—a craving for the unknown and the vast, which spread itself vaguely and perhaps unattainably before his imagination—his disappointments very naturally vexed him somewhat beyond prudence, and now and then beyond the restraint of right reason. He usually came to a knowledge of his error before it had led too far, and his repentance then was not less ready than his wrong. So in the present instance. . . . He strove to forget the feelings of the jealous and disappointed lover, in the lately recollected duties of the man and citizen (375).

This portrait is a foreshadowing of a whole gallery of young Southern heroes yet to come. Their fieriness of character Simms saw as both a virtue and a potential menace, but the trait seemed to him inherent in the Southern nature.[8] When he sought later an effective way to counterbalance it—to make the hothead less selfish and more aware of his social responsibilities—he was led to the creation of his most original character: the scout, or frontiersman. As I have already indicated in Chapter I, it was to be the scout's function to tone down the young man's devil-may-care schemes, to deflate his posturing and his high-flown rhetoric through the earthy language of the border. Such a catalyst had been dimly suggested in Mark Forrester of *Guy Rivers*, but Simms did not follow him with a corresponding figure in *The Yemassee* since it is Harrison who exercises this influence upon Hugh.

Considering Harrison and Hugh together, we may observe further that Simms has each man display active revulsion against Puritanism (and its New England associations) as it is represented by old Matthews and by Grayson's mother. Though Simms respected Christianity as a moral force, he was never a formal member of a church, and he came to loathe the narrowness of Southern fundamentalism. To Simms such a religious attitude put a check upon the free spirit; and, left unopposed, it was apt to undercut an established hierarchy. Simms dramatizes this danger through Matthews, who "was a bigot himself, and, with the power, would doubtless have tyrannised after a similar fashion" (62). Morality and religion were to be matters for the individual and were not to be impressed upon him. To the leader, both came naturally through heredity and a cultured environment; through his own character development he inspired the lower ranks. Simms was not to forget this stand for the individual's right to interpret religion when he had to face the issue of the morality of slavery.

When we consider the second level of the society represented in *The Yemassee*, we may note that in a tale set in the time before full development of towns and plantations Simms could not present a very wide range of occupations. Moreover, only a few of the members of the cast have the chance during the rigors of the plot to exhibit much individuality. Among the ones who do is Dr. Nichols, a comic bore who is a cousin of similar types found in Cooper. Nichols has another and more dangerous side: he is a demagogue always itching to harangue the people but not at all ready to undergo the danger which leadership entails. As Simms presents him, he wants "popular rights" without incurring any of the duties himself; totally hypocritical as a "leader," he has to be suppressed.

Another person who manages to stand out is Mrs. Granger, wife of a man who has been a trader among the Yemassees. Mrs. Granger is fully rendered as the Southern frontier woman, a figure never to rise to a position of authority but one who was playing a vital role in the South's growth. Schooled in hardship, Mrs. Granger is well qualified to cope with the wilderness; as Simms comments, her mind

> grew strong in proportion to its trials, and she had learned, in the end, to regard them with a degree of fearlessness far beyond the capacities of any well-bred heir of prosperity and favouring fortune. . . . She counselled [her husband's] enterprises, prompted or persuaded his proceedings, managed for him wisely and economically; in all respects, proved herself unselfish; and, if she did not at any time appear above the way of life they had adopted, she took care to maintain both of them from falling beneath it . . . (367-68).

It is this type, Simms urges, that society must have in its middle classes: a woman strong, adaptable, and not too sensitive—one willing to accept responsibility when required (as she does in the culminating fight at the Block House) but otherwise content to remain in her secondary station.

Akin to Mrs. Granger in personal integrity but otherwise poles apart, is Bess Matthews, the destined bride of the hero. Like every other beautiful, virginal, intelligent heroine of this period of American fiction, Bess strikes us as having been constructed of some chemical compound known only to novelists. In *The Yemassee* she is Virtue, the prototype of Ideal Southern Womanhood, the ordained Mother of a Noble Race. As a plot device, she is Virtue to be rescued from Distress—the prey of Indian, prurient white, and even beady-eyed rattlesnake. It is easy to laugh at her type, less easy to see how the writer of romance could have resolved the dilemma her character presented. As a maiden, she had to project simultaneously the aura of innocence and of physical allurement; after marriage, by the literary convention of the time, the subject of her awakened sexual status could only be hinted at. How a *lady* could also be a wife to a normal male was a problem that appears to have bothered the idealizing Southerner outside of fiction as well—but that is another story. Within the romance, Simms employed the usual compromise: the heroine as major character vanishes at the altar, to reappear (if at all) mature and beyond further love interest.

There remains, in our survey of the social orders represented in *The Yemassee*, the third and lowest class. The renegade or outcast is melodramatically present in the persons of Richard Chorley and his piratical crew, who have been commissioned by the Spaniards of Florida to give aid to the Yemassees in their war against the British. Since the whole crowd is eventually wiped out, it is clear that Simms is indicating that such people had to be removed before society could perfect itself. Like the Indian, the outlaw is neither stable enough to be raised up nor willing himself to remain in a subordinate position.

The broad base of Southern civilization was, then, inevitably to be the Negroes; and even in 1835 Simms was sly enough to insert a testimonial to the slave system in Hector, the body servant of Harrison. Hector's functions (aside from muddling the plot) are dual: he provides in speech and action traditional comic relief; and, in a scene in which Harrison attempts to give him his freedom, he allows Simms an opening for the earliest direct defense of slavery in his fiction. The comic scenes are done in the irritating "Sambo" strain that was to deface American writing for years, but Hector is not created as a simple figure of fun. Brave if stupid, honest, devotedly loyal to Harrison, Hector is Simms's own idea of what a slave must be under an enlightened owner. The passage in which Harrison tries to reward him because Hector has saved his life makes its point through the words of the slave himself:

> "Yes, Hector,—you are now free. [Harrison is speaking] I give you your freedom, old fellow. Here is money, too, and in Charleston you shall have a house to live in for yourself."
>
> "No, maussa; I can't go; I can't be free," replied the negro. . . .
>
> "Why can't you, Hector? What do you mean? Am I not your master? Can't I make you free, and don't I tell you that I do make you free? From this moment you are your own master."
>
> "Wha' for, maussa? Wha' Hector done, you guine turn um off dis time o' day?"
>
> "Done! You have saved my life, old fellow—you have fought for me like a friend, and I am now your friend, and not any longer your master."

This notion is too socially advanced for Hector:

> "I d—n to h-ll, maussa, if I guine to be free!" roared the adhesive black, in a tone of unrestrainable determination. "I can't

loss you company. . . . 'Tis onpossible, maussa, and dere's no
use for talk 'bout it. De ting ain't right: and enty I know wha'
kind of thing freedom is wid black man? Ha! you make Hector
free, he turn wuss more nor poor buckrah—he tief out of de
shop—he git drunk and lie in de ditch—den, if sick come, he roll,
he toss in de wet grass of de stable. . . . No, maussa—you and
Dugdale [Harrison's dog] berry good company for Hector. I tank
God he so good—I no want any better" (437-38).

This scene is slightly anachronistic for its presumed time of
1715; in his dialect, in his reference to shop, ditch, and stable,
Hector sounds much more like the plantation hand of Simms's
own day than like the servant of an eighteenth-century lord.
But by 1835 the abolitionist movement was afoot, and Simms had
his eye on the coming challenge. He was not as yet a violent
Southern nationalist but rather a committed sectionalist; and in
The Yemassee he discovered his method of defending the South
by positive statement about its virtues instead of direct retort to
Northern agitators.

In sum, *The Yemassee* was a major advance in Simms's career
in fiction, despite the continuing faults of careless writing and
romantic cliché. As contemporary readers commented, it told
an exciting story and its suspense was competently handled—but
in these respects it did not differ markedly from many other
popular romances. What makes *The Yemassee* notable, in retro-
spect, is that it opened up for Simms his concept of an "epic
age" in the South. It was an idea that he was to carry forward
in detail in the series of Revolutionary romances; and he was to
undertake its expansion in the very next romance he wrote,
The Partisan.

CHAPTER 4

The Epic Struggle

I *Revolutionaries and King's Men*

FROM THE DAY of its publication *The Yemassee* attracted an enthusiastic band of admirers. As Simms recalled later, "The New York papers spoke of it in one language of commendation" (*L*, II, 226); and several critics pronounced his handling of the Indian superior to Cooper's.[1] But, despite what must have been his satisfaction in this recognition, Simms did not again employ the Indian as major character for many years. Another—though not totally unrelated—topic was now dominating his mind, and before he was done it had run its course in seven long books. That subject was the American Revolution as fought in the Southern colonies, particularly the guerilla or "partisan" warfare in South Carolina.[2]

The war was an almost perfect motif for Simms to hit upon, for it permitted him to combine his sober interest in fact with the romancer's delight in legend and tradition. Recollecting in his preface a recent visit to a village that had figured in the conflict, Simms commented upon the dual interest that had generated the basic notion of *The Partisan:*

> It was while thus rambling among the ruins of the place, that my imagination grew active in the contemplation of objects so well calculated to stimulate its exercise. Memory came warmly and vividly to its aid, and recalled a series of little events, carefully treasured up by the local tradition, which, unconsciously, my mind began to throw together, and to combine in form. Some of these had long before ministered to my own pleasurable emotions—why should they not yield similar pleasure to others? . . . The design grew more familiar and more feasible, the more

I contemplated it. . . . To these circumstances, and to this desire, "The Partisan" owes its origin.[3]

This statement, though a public utterance and one composed some time after the fact, is strikingly revelatory of Simms's general method in the Revolutionary romances. After experiencing the emotions of sentimentality and melancholy evoked by his actual walk through the "ancient" ruins of the village of Dorchester, he proceeds to mull over the historical facts and the legends already familiar to him. These stimulate a strong feeling of local pride as he recalls the deeds of heroism enacted, and, suddenly, the whole idea of the Revolution as the South's most "heroic" period is before him—what he calls "the most perilous and the most brilliant crisis of our fortunes" (xi). Personal emotion is the primary stimulus, not the historian's desire to collect and arrange factual data. Though Simms prided himself upon the accuracy of the historical background in his fiction, it was what he devised in the foreground—the local scenes, the creation and analysis of typically Southern characters— that gave his books their special quality. As was true of *The Yemassee, The Partisan* (1835) was a reconstruction of the past as an exemplar for the present. It was as if Simms were saying to his countrymen: "These people of the Revolution were your own ancestors. In your present difficulties and in the possible conflicts that lie ahead, look on their deeds and emulate their courage."

It follows that for Simms the most significant actors in his saga of revolution were the leaders, the small band of representatives of the old families who organized an underground movement against the occupying British forces. Simms's own angle of vision must be understood, for many readers are apt to see in his proud old colonels and stiff young majors only his ready submission to the conventions of romance. These "conventional" aristocrats, however, are more carefully drawn and differentiated than is commonly admitted; Simms makes them stand, in their various ways, for certain problems in the Southern character.

To demonstrate how Simms develops these problems, it is necessary first to detail something of the historical situation at the time *The Partisan* opens. The year is 1780 and Charleston has fallen to British arms; a further defeat for the Americans lies just ahead at Camden, and everywhere in the lower South the patriots' cause is in jeopardy. Moreover, the British commandant has issued a proclamation nullifying all the paroles (agreements of protection) which had been granted to certain Americans who promised not to hinder the invaders; all these Carolinians are expected to join the king's troops and to stop the Americans moving southward under General Gates. What will those who have relied upon neutrality do? Can they be forced to fight against their own countrymen? Simms makes this issue of conflicting loyalties the central theme of *The Partisan;* and he presents it dramatically by contrasting a South Carolina patriarch, Colonel Walton, with his nephew, Major Robert Singleton, a partisan leader who is under the command of Marion the "Swamp Fox."

Colonel Walton is one of those Americans who had agreed to the original terms for becoming a noncombatant. He is no coward, but he believes the British will restore order without further molestation of the Carolinians and he is not convinced that the Americans could ever drive out the foreign invaders. A "gentleman in every sense of the word" (117), he has retired to his ancestral plantation, enjoying as of old its civilized pleasures.

Major Singleton, though, has refused any compromise. In outward appearance he is another bundle of romantic platitudes: his face is "finely intelligent and tolerably handsome"; his person is "symmetry itself"; and, crowning all, is that inevitable "clustering brown hair" (21). But Singleton has an important thematic function to fulfill, and in this role he almost makes us forget the derivativeness of his noble figure. As the new leader of a partisan band he despises his uncle's life of inaction; he cannot rest until he has talked the old man into returning to the cause. On a visit to the plantation, both to see the colonel's daughter and to persuade him to accept a commission offered by Marion, Singleton forces their two points of view into an open debate.

After a warm exchange during which he comes close to impugning the colonel's bravery, he brings up Marion's offer and is gratified to have it accepted. But the colonel has one reservation that almost wrecks all he has done to restore his honor. Recognizing that his decision means that his lands will now be open to confiscation by the British, the colonel mourns: " 'I have a strange love for these old groves—this family mansion, descended to me like a sacred trust through so many hands and ancestors. I would not that they should be lost' " (163).

The rejoinder of Singleton, who has lost his own home to the enemy, is crushing: " 'Now, by heaven, uncle, had I known of this—had I dreamed that thou hadst weighed, for an instant, the fine sense of honour in the scales against thy love of this thy dwelling-place—my own hand should have applied the torch to its shingles. . . . I would have shouted in triumph, that I saved you from the dishonourable bargain which you have made for [the estate's] protection so long' " (163).

In spite of this stage rhetoric, Singleton does convey Simms's serious meaning: To be a leader and to enjoy the concomitant benefits, one must continue to *deserve* to lead. Power and possessions cannot be retained unless the leader accepts the fact that they carry a moral responsibility. If he fails to acknowledge his duties, then things become mere ends in themselves; and the social structure is given a dangerous shake.

This theme of individual responsibility is also borne by Katharine, the colonel's daughter, who is Singleton's sweetheart. Her role is somewhat limited in *The Partisan* (she appears again in later volumes of the series), but a few of her speeches establish the deep integrity of true Southern womanhood. We are not surprised when Simms advises us that she is "stately and beautiful," "one of those high-souled creatures that awe while they attract" (104), but rather unexpectedly she is also a political actionist. Unswervingly on the side of the colonials, she has been daringly free in airing her feelings to British officers who have visited the plantation while her father accepted protection. When one of them mooningly tells her that he can never be an enemy to her, she does all but spit on him: "I am a Southron, sir," she proudly proclaims; "one of a people not apt to suffer wrong to their friends or kindred, without resenting and resisting it" (289). She says "Southron" and not "American"; just as Singleton is Southern Leader as well as conventional hero, so Katharine as heroine embodies the pride in region and station that makes her a proper consort.

Set directly against Katharine's sprightly patriotism are the meek religiosity and frailty of her cousin Emily (Singleton's sister), who has taken refuge from the strife as a guest in Colonel Walton's plantation home. Doomed (for chapters) to waste away of consumption, this pale, attractive girl furnishes a choice sample of the period's addiction to weeping sentimentality. Like Dickens, Simms knew the sale value of the tear-jerker; in *The Partisan* he perceived also the necessity for providing some emotional relief from the general heroics. But the scene in Emily's death chamber, with its angels and yawning heavenly gates, is simply emotionally awash; as Oscar Wilde once remarked of the death of Dickens' Little Nell, it would take a heart of stone not to laugh at it. Simms does make a diffident attempt to give a bit of stiffening to Emily's backbone by having her rail at the war in which her family is taking part; in the story she alone cries out against both sides, condemning battle as "hateful to one professing the Christian faith" (272). But even here Emily falters; she concedes to her brother that a nation should not submit to tyranny. Simms fails because he wants to have it both ways: to give due respect to the religious pacifist viewpoint, but also to haul the reader back by assuring him that the cause is nevertheless just.[4]

Colonel Walton, Singleton, Katharine, and Emily are all representatives of the aristocratic class in *The Partisan,* but Simms varies their personalities enough to show that there is interplay within that rank. This same sort of healthy diversity he also depicts among the class that must be led. He gathers several of these types into the band of partisans which Singleton conducts on forays; his closest aides—the shrewd William Humphries, the adolescent Lance Frampton, and the volatile John Davis—are all patriotic men of the countryside who are knowledgeable but in need of guidance. Thus far they have had their minor successes against the British, Simms implies, because they recognize their stations and are willing to take orders from above. Warm in spirit (sometimes to manly excess), courageous, unlettered, but alert, they are sharpened by their commander, just as they help to draw out his highborn qualities. This interaction between leader and led is best expressed in a scene in which Singleton prepares his men for a raid. Like Henry V before Agincourt (the verbal echoes of Shakespeare's play are obvious), he makes the rounds of the troop:

[H]e had his friendly word for all. . . . No person, however humble, went utterly unnoticed. . . . And there was no effort in this familiar frankness, and no air of condescension. He was a man speaking to men; and did not appear to dream of any necessity of making every word, look, and tone remind them of his authority. His bearing, when not engaged in the absolute duties of the service, was that of an equal, simply. And yet there was really no familiarity between the parties. . . . When he addressed them, he did so with great respect, which always tutored them when they spoke to him. . . . Yet nobody ever thought of accusing Singleton of pride. His gentleness of manner, ease and grace and frankness of speech, were proverbial among his men. Truly, he was the man to be a leader of southern woodsmen (355-56).

Somewhere in between Singleton and his men stands the character who has been cited as Simms's most striking individual creation, Lieutenant Porgy. Porgy has a much larger part in some of the later installments (notably *Woodcraft*), but he requires at least a glance here. Since he is a fabulous but epicurean eater, a lover of conviviality, a spinner of verbal fancies, and is gross in body (though not in mind), he has reminded nearly every reader of Shakespeare's Falstaff.[5] But the resemblance is only a superficial one, and insistence upon it only obscures Simms's basic intention in creating him. Certainly Porgy is no fat knight to Singleton's Prince Hal; there are only a few meetings between them in *The Partisan*, but at no point does the major treat his lieutenant as a butt for jest or cast doubt upon his essential bravery. Porgy is, as Simms tells us several times, "eminently a gentleman"; and he warns us not to misinterpret his role:

If we have said or shown anything calculated to lessen his dignity in the eyes of any of our readers, remorse must follow. Porgy might *play* the buffoon, if he pleased; but in the mean time, let it be understood, that he was born to wealth, and had received the education of a gentleman. He had wasted his substance, perhaps, but this matter does not much concern us now. It is only important that he should not be supposed to waste himself. He had been a planter—was, in some measure, a planter still, with broken fortunes, upon the Ashepoo. . . . He was a sort of laughing philosopher, who, as if in anticipation of the free speech of others, dealt with himself as little mercifully as his nearest friends might have done . . . [358-59].

Porgy is an unusual type in the Simms canon: he is the relaxed aristocrat, the gentleman who, because of personal inclination, has chosen to place himself just below the more sober-minded leaders. In some of his actions and in his speech he reveals the sort of man that Simms conceived himself to be;[6] and while he is not a serious person, he is meant to be taken seriously. The story of his postwar experiences fills one whole book (*Woodcraft*); and his character offers enough complexities to justify further commentary in each of his other appearances.

Of the "low" figures in the cast, only a few need any mention. Tom, Porgy's Negro cook who travels with him, is portrayed much as is Harrison's Hector: there is the same friendship between master and slave—and the same social gulf. Some of the other minor characters illustrate Simms's continuing bondage to earlier Gothic fiction, his old delight in the bizarre and melodramatic. "Goggle" Blonay, a repellent part-Indian who sells out to the British, is an unbelievable villain who curses his illegitimate birth in the spirit (if not in the language) of Shakespeare's bastards; his mother, a poor-white who dabbles in charms and potions, is quite rightly thought a witch by her neighbors—though she is patently an inept one. Since "Goggle" figures more positively in important scenes in the next volume of the series (*Mellichampe*), he will be considered with that book.

In the later chapters of *The Partisan* Simms abruptly takes the reader away from the border fighting to the historical battle of Camden; and the story loses a good bit of its drive as he turns to an analysis of the actions of Cornwallis, Gates, Tarleton, DeKalb, and other officers on both sides. His own personal absorption in this American defeat even spurred him to the inclusion of long documents—like Gates's general battle order in Chapter 42—and to the recounting of the engagement as a historian and not as a romancer. There is some recovery in the closing action, in which Singleton manages to rescue Colonel Walton from a band of Britons set to hang him as a traitor. But the story as a whole trails off with Simms's promise of a sequel; the tale lacks the sense of roundness, of a finished action, that he had achieved in *The Yemassee*. As Simms himself saw, in a comment written some years after the book's appearance, "the design was feeble, the parts clumsily put together. . . . Wherever the *action* was in progress, the story told, but there were frequent breaks & lapses, which spoiled the effect" (*L*, II, 229).

This analysis is sound, but *The Partisan* does have positive merits. Simms was experimenting more with letting conflict grow naturally out of character—as in the scenes between Singleton and Colonel Walton—and he was more sparing in his use of the device of the rescuing angel. He treated the British fairly and not as brutal automatons; he had them exhibit loutishness only when there was recorded fact to support the scene, and he showed many of them merely as professional soldiers engaged to do a job. If the figures of Emily and the Blonays were the product of intellectual flabbiness, he was able to offset them to a degree with the more original Porgy.

It is true that Poe, reviewing *The Partisan* for the *Southern Literary Messenger,* found Porgy a "most insufferable bore"; and Singleton he signalized as "about as much of a nonentity as most other heroes of our acquaintance." But he concluded that the book as a whole was "no ordinary work" and recommended its historical details as "replete with interest."[7] Other critics were to give the tale mixed notices, but most of them were now agreed that Simms's talent had to be reckoned with seriously.

II *Recapitulation*

Within the space of two years Simms had published one work of fiction in each of the three fields that were long associated with his name: the contemporary Southern border, the colonial period, and the Revolutionary War. These thematic distinctions were conventional in his own day, and they have remained convenient in discussing the body of his romances. But I would re-emphasize that *Guy Rivers, The Yemassee,* and *The Partisan* are in a fundamental sense all border tales. The modern reader who finds in Simms only the dreary repetition of standard plot device may miss this important point: the real subject of all his best work is the interaction between civilization and frontier. No critic, certainly, should deny that one of Simms's aims was to hold his audience's attention and that he often employed crude and obvious methods of doing so. Nor should the critic be reluctant to admit that these books are filled with puerilities of diction and style.

For it can be properly added that what raises Simms's romances above the dusty heap of the period's second-rate fiction is his theme of the South—a theme not duplicated in detail by any other American writer before the Civil War. Far more than has been appreciated, he was concerned with the roles his characters played in a unique American society; he studied—not as a sociologist but as a maker of myth—how Southern types came into being and how they went about constructing a social order. At first, in *Martin Faber* and in *Guy Rivers,* he experimented with a method quite alien to his temperament, psychological analysis based on the practice of Godwin and Bulwer. Others among his fictional creations—like Harrison, Walton, and Singleton—also picked up their costumes in the novelist's storehouse; but by late 1835 Simms was associating them with living types of the South and was endeavoring to give to them a symbolic status.

Thus far Simms's performance had clearly been uneven; and the questions that these books pose have been brought up about all his fiction. Were their stronger elements the "realistic"—or the "romantic"? Did he succeed better with low characters like "Goggle" and Chorley the pirate—or with heroes like Harrison? Ought we to agree, with one recent critic, that we should "endure" the gallants and their lady loves because we know that Simms will soon take us on the road to the backwoods again? (*L*, I, xlvii).

As I have indicated, something can be said for both positions. But in my discussions of his later tales I will be concerned to establish that many of these questions are actually irrelevant, that they stem simply from our ignorance of the form that Simms said he was practicing in *The Yemassee*—the American romance.

CHAPTER 5

The Avenger of Blood

I *Feuds in the Swamp*

THE LABOR of rapidly composing and seeing three long works of fiction through the press exhausted Simms for a time and brought on doubts and emotional upsets. Harassed as usual by financial problems, overburdened by the strain of constantly grinding out copy for periodicals, he could not force himself to the irritating task of careful revision; and he feared that *The Partisan* might not receive the complimentary press notices his last two books had won. In this darkened mood, he wrote his friend Lawson that a real failure would set him back seriously and that he would then consider retiring from the field. Typically, he added: "I have been busy upon a sequel to 'The Partisan' which I am pleased with"; however, his new doubts nagged at him once more and he completed the sentence: "but I begin to distrust my own judgment dreadfully, and there is surely no worse sign than this" (*L*, I, 80).

The reception of *The Partisan* was more gentle than Simms appears in this letter to have expected, and he found no real cause to lay down his pen. But one critic suggested that the story had been left unfinished and that the low characters were given too much prominence, and these charges nettled him. When his second Revolutionary romance, *Mellichampe*, appeared late in 1836, he quoted some of the unfavorable comments and laid into his detractors. The first charge—that the story trailed off—he dismissed as meaningless since he had made it clear he was planning a series. And to the second quibble—that there were too many vulgarians—he rejoined:

The question first occurs, "Does the story profess to belong to a country and to a period of history which are alike known—and does it misrepresent either?" If it does not, the objection will not lie. . . . My object usually has been to adhere, as closely as possible, to the features and the attributes of real life, as it is to be found in the precise scenes, and under the governing circumstances—some of them extraordinary and romantic, because new—in which my narrative has followed it. . . .[1]

Here Simms's pride in his creation of "new" characters and his confidence in his method seem restored, and in the tale which follows he baits his critics by providing more of the same fare which had gagged them.

Mellichampe may best be described in Simms's own words as "a sort of continuation of, but not a sequel" to *The Partisan* (*L*, I, 89). That is, though it employs many of the same characters and resolves at least one of the minor plots, it does not press to a conclusion the Singleton-Katharine Walton love story which had been central to the previous volume. In a way it is an interlude in Simms's larger plan to present the whole story of the major campaigns in the South since it deals with no major historical events and concerns itself largely (so far as the war goes) with the raids of Singleton's partisans.

The plot line is—for Simms—comparatively simple, being constructed around two blood feuds and their outcomes. The more important of these is the hostility which has developed between Ernest Mellichampe, another quick-tempered young aristocrat, and a Tory named Barsfield, who has been rewarded with the Mellichampe estate after he has slain Ernest's father and has confiscated his property for the British. The second of the quarrels stems directly from minor events in *The Partisan*. Singleton's aide Humphries has come to hate "Goggle" Blonay because old Mother Blonay had attempted to aid a British officer in the seduction of Humphries' sister. Blonay has even better reasons: he is gunning for Humphries because the latter had accidentally ridden down and killed Mother Blonay during the raid which saved Colonel Walton.

This second subplot, with its reminiscences of melodrama and Gothic tale, could easily be skimmed over were it not for its important evidence of Simms's concept of the Southern code of fair conduct. Moreover, its culminating scene is not only one of the best that Simms invented but also—as one critic has said— "one of the most moving in frontier literature" (*L*, I, xliv).

This is the episode in which Humphries, having been relentlessly tracked by the half-breed "Goggle" for some days, manages to catch him hiding in a hollow cypress and pens him up by stuffing the opening with branches. This deed may remind one of wicked barons walling up their enemies in castle recesses, but actually it deserves credit as an example of the sort of use of native materials that Charles Brockden Brown had urged in his preface to *Edgar Huntly*. Brown himself might have approved the evocation of Humphries' emotional state at the close of the incident:

> He was at last secure from the hunter of blood—he had triumphed—and yet he could not keep down the fancy, which continually, as he went, imbodied the supposed cries of the half-breed in little gusts of wind, that seemed to pursue him; and, when he emerged from the wood, a strange chill went through his bones, and he looked back momently, even when the gigantic cypress, which was the sepulchre of his enemy, no longer reared up its solemn spire in his sight. It was no longer behind him. It seemed to move before him faster than his horse; and he spurred the animal furiously forward, seeking to pass the fast-travelling tree, and to escape the moaning sound which came after him upon the breeze [381].

Humphries is a hardened fighter, with no fear of killing or of being killed; but leaving a fellow human to such a death conflicts with his sense of justice. Unable to still his conscience, he returns next day to the tree, frees his captive, and says to him: "'I had you safe enough, but I couldn't find it in my heart to take your life after that fashion, so I let you out. Tell me, now, if you can go without taking tracks after me again?'" (406). Blonay will not promise, and Humphries has no choice but to offer to duel with him. But, as he quickly sees, Blonay's hand has been crushed; he would be unable to use his rifle. And so he sends him away, reflecting: "'You're from my own parish, and that's one reason . . . why I want to give you fair play, and it's reason enough why I don't want to spill your blood.'" Blonay has to be dispatched later in the story because he is a villain and a turncoat, but he dies in a fight in which he takes the chances of combat in the open. Simms permits neither him nor Humphries to resolve a blood feud by means of unfair advantage.

This theme of a proper code of behavior between antagonists also underlies the Mellichampe-Barsfield quarrel, though the rash Mellichampe must constantly be reminded of his duty by the scout Thumbscrew Witherspoon, who is his constant companion. Mellichampe, nearly maddened by the death of his father, is imperiling his honor because he wishes to slay Barsfield on sight. But Thumbscrew, like Humphries a product of the frontier, chastens him and forces him to face the issue: if one's intended victim does not have a chance of defense, the act of killing him can be a crime worse than whatever provoked the hostility.

A lengthy debate between Thumbscrew and Mellichampe gives dramatic force to Simms's notion of this code. Young Mellichampe, frothing over his wrongs, has become an avenger of blood and has lost sight of the larger conflict in which his father died. So when Thumbscrew reports that he has seen Barsfield passing through the woods and has not ambushed him, Mellichampe berates the scout for cowardly inaction: " 'I am not more quick or impatient, . . . than a man should be in such a case. Not to be quick when one is wronged, is to invite injustice. . . . I know no good that comes of submission, except to make tyrants and slaves; and I tell you, . . . I shall never submit to the one, nor be the other' " (34).

But Thumbscrew knows that, though the sentiment sounds manly, it is morally dangerous. First, however, he tries to placate his friend: " 'A mighty fine spirit, Airnest, and to speak what's gospel true, I like it myself. . . . I'm not a man myself to let another play tantrums with me; and, for sartain, I sha'n't find fault with them that's most like myself in that partic'lar . . .' " (34). And yet, he goes on:

> "My idee is, that fighting is the part of a beast-brute, and not for a true-born man, that has a respect for himself, and knows what's good-breeding; and I only fights when there's brutes standing waiting for it. Soon as a man squints at me as if he was going to play the beast with me, by the eternal splinters, I'll mount him, lick or no lick, and do my best, tooth, tusk, and grinders to astonish him. But afore that, I'm peaceable as a pine stump, lying quiet in my own bush. . . . Now, though I do say you're to keep quiet, and lie snug at the present, that

isn't to say that you're to do nothing. No, no—you're to get in readiness for what's to come, and not be wanting when you have a chance to turn your enemy upon his back. It a'n't revenge, but it's justice, and my lawful, natural right, that I fights for . . ." (34, 37).

The whole scene, neatly balanced between the impassioned rhetoric of Mellichampe and the colloquial diction of the common-sensical woodsman, is a critical one for apprehending Simms's conception of both classes. Ernest Mellichampe is as well born and as nobly handsome as any of Simms's previous heroes. But is he fit to be a leader? Not, the episode reveals, until he has rid himself of the flaw of believing that any action is in itself a virtue. As the two men argue, we watch the interplay of civilization and frontier that Simms believed was necessary for bringing out the best in each level of society. Because of his heredity and education Mellichampe is qualified to command as the frontiersman can never be. But Thumbscrew has a balancing noble quality of his own: "It a'n't revenge, but it's justice . . . that I fights for."

In this first important appearance of the woodsman, Simms extended the doctrines he had only hinted at in his three preceding romances, and he was to return several times to the theme of frontier influence. Through Thumbscrew, who eventually dies for him, Mellichampe learns the lesson of self-control and comes to accept responsibility for the effects his actions will have upon others. When he does, he sees that the Revolution—group combat for a national cause—is of far greater importance than his own desire for personal revenge.

This is a lesson which Mellichampe's beloved, Janet Berkeley, does not have to be taught. Janet's father is a timid and ineffectual gentleman who admits Barsfield and his British retinue to his estate because he wants to show no favoritism. But the old virtues he has lost live on in his patriotic daughter. To be sure, she is brought on stage in terms as fulsomely sentimental as Simms had used to introduce his other heroines, but Janet comes off better as a person because she is allowed a larger share in the action. Like Katharine Walton she is a suitable mate for a leader; but, unlike Katharine, she finds she must contribute some of her own steadiness to her lover. She is even a good tactician. After Barsfield and his cronies have taken over the Berkeley estate, she and her father join the partisan band; and it is she who discovers the means for a counterattack. Coming across a bow and some fire arrows in their overseer's house, she sends them to Major Singleton with the direction that he use them to set the mansion ablaze and flush the enemy: "'Take the arrows, and do not let the hand tremble and the eye turn aside when you direct them to that sacred roof; it is now devoted to our country . . .'" (197).

Janet nearly always talks in this lofty way; and in her cloying love scenes with Mellichampe she totally alienates the modern reader. It is indeed difficult in our day to understand why Simms gave her dialogue like this: "'If I sought for mere pleasure and amusement in love, I might tire of its sameness; but the love of my heart is its devotion, and the better feelings of our nature, like the God from which they come, are the more dear to us, and the more lovely in his sight, as they are never subject to change'" (324).

"Beautiful sentiment!" cries Mellichampe—and he is off on a flight of his own. But his words suggest a way to read such violet passages. For Mellichampe and Janet are not only exchanging protestations of their love: they are playing a complicated rhetorical game as well. This game of "beautiful sentiments" seems to have remained in vogue longer in the South than in other parts of the country, and it is amusing to reflect that Simms and his own betrothed may have been experts at it since he was preparing to remarry that year. It will not do, of course, to try to restore these passages on any grounds of "realism"; the absurd cult of sensibility can never be taken seriously again. But it may be useful, in attempting to grasp Simms's picture of the South he knew, to realize that living people actually could "talk like a book."

Since Simms concentrates in *Mellichampe* upon the two blood feuds and upon the love affair, few of the other characters among the patriots warrant much discussion. Singleton and his band are always lurking somewhere in the background, and Porgy too makes a brief reappearance—apparently simply because he had proved popular with readers of *The Partisan*.[2] And once again we find a Negro who saves his master and gains Simms's praise:

> Scipio was one of those trusty slaves to be found in almost every native southern family, who, having grown up with the children of their owners, have acquired a certain correspondence of feeling with them. A personal attachment had strengthened the bonds which necessity imposed, and it was quite as much a principle in Scipio's mind to fight and die for his owners, as to work for them . . . [104].

Of the figures arrayed on the enemy side, the Tory Barsfield receives somewhat unexpected treatment. Though he is fated to die because he has killed old Mellichampe, he is not a thoroughly unsympathetic character. In a long talk with Janet (whom he wants to marry) he reveals why he—a Southerner too— had refused to join his neighbors and had turned instead to the British. At the beginning of the war, he tells her, he had declined a role on either side; but a band of Whigs, under old Mellichampe, had threatened him and finally tarred and feathered him. And why did they act thus? he asks Janet. "'I was punished . . . for a crime so monstrous as that of thinking differently from my neighbor,'" he comments bitterly. "'Hence it is, that I am a tory'" (313-14).

Simms allows Barsfield his say in order to maintain a reasonable balance between the opposing sides. Just as the revolutionists are not all spotless but confuse their private passions with the conduct of the war, so their antagonists are not saturated with black. As Simms points out in his preface, the Revolution was fought by men, and there were errors and injustices by both parties. But if he makes this concession, he is also anxious to suggest that these were deviations from a proper *norm* of conduct.

As an entity, *Mellichampe* is a more relaxed and "domestic" romance than either *The Yemassee* or *The Partisan;* no great actions are undertaken and the scope is considerably reduced. But if it is essentially an interlude, it remains important for Simms's adding to his panorama of the South the full portraits of three who enrich its meaning: Mellichampe, Thumbscrew, and Barsfield.

II *Bandits on the Border*

Mellichampe garnered fair reviews, but Simms for a time turned his attention to subjects outside the South; and the period between this second Revolutionary story and *Richard*

Hurdis (1838), the second of the border romances, was an undistinguished one. Not that he was inactive: both his private and his professional interests fully occupied his days. In the autumn of 1836 he married Chevillette Eliza Roach, daughter of a planter who owned properties along the Edisto River, and the couple took up permanent residence at the plantation of "Woodlands."[3] The summer of the following year Simms and his bride spent in the New England mountains, where he busied himself with several literary projects: a foreign romance, *Pelayo;* a verse tragedy which he hoped to induce the actor Edwin Forrest to accept; and the long review of Harriet Martineau's *Society in America* which has been examined in Chapter I.

The tragedy did not come off, and the foreign romance merits almost no notice at all. *Pelayo,* a tedious tale of Spain reworked from a dramatic poem he had written in his youth, is entirely derivative; and a sequel to it, *Count Julian,* is, if possible, worse.[4] The only interest they can now arouse in a reader is the question as to why he wanted to write them. It is likely that Simms wished to try his hand at the sort of European tale that his rival Cooper had recently been turning out; it is also possible, as W. P. Trent suggests, that Simms's friends had urged him to dismiss the comparatively youthful South for "a more ancient and foreign and, therefore, more dignified theme."[5] However, no matter what prompted them, the Spanish romances were artistic and financial disasters; and Simms finally conceded his mistake by omitting them from his collected edition.

Though he was, stubbornly, to sneak back to foreign settings in a few other tales, he quickly switched to the South again in 1838, when he published a "tale of Alabama," *Richard Hurdis; or, The Avenger of Blood.* Like *Guy Rivers,* this second border romance has a contemporary subject; but, unlike the earlier book, it shows less reliance on fictional models, and hews more directly to a central situation. The main plot deals with a "Mystic Brotherhood" of frontier outlaws, an idea suggested to Simms by the activities of John A. Murrell, a gang leader who roamed in Alabama and Mississippi and who only recently had been brought to justice. In the preface to the revised version of this romance, Simms claimed direct knowledge of Murrell's activities, asserting that he had "met certain of the *dramatis personae* during my early wanderings in that then wild country."[6]

Undoubtedly he drew from his personal adventures in the border states, but he also had a look at several books about the depredations of this "land pirate."[7] The whole tale, then, is a blend of reminiscence, factual detail, and purely imaginative additions.

Like *Mellichampe*, *Richard Hurdis* is partly concerned with a revenge motif. Richard, the restless and rash young hero, has been contesting with his quiet but criminally inclined brother John for the affections of Mary Easterby, who is all that Simms's other young Southern ladies are. As the story begins, Richard, mistakenly convinced that Mary prefers John, seeks exile in the Indian "nation." With him travels William Carrington, a lighthearted friend who is off to collect a debt from a back-woods settler, Matt Webber. Webber, we find, is a member of a secret band of outlaws who prey on travelers and steal slaves for resale; so, when Richard and William call upon him, he takes them captive in hopes of booty. William escapes, but is shot down by mistake by Ben Pickett, a worthless squatter hired by John Hurdis to murder Richard because John has now learned Mary prefers his rival.

Richard is eventually freed by Colonel Grafton, an old family friend; and the remainder of the story is given to Richard's attempt to avenge the murder of William and to his discovery that his brother is his blood enemy. At first Richard blames the outlaw gang for the slaying, and in disguise he works his way into the secret councils of the "brotherhood." Meanwhile, Webber hears that John Hurdis had sent Pickett to kill Richard, and he blackmails them both into becoming reluctant members of the gang. With this complication set up, Simms moves rapidly to the climax. Richard, with Colonel Grafton's aid, rounds up a posse and wipes out the band of brigands, including his brother, whose fratricidal plot he now learns in full. Only the gang leader, Clement Foster (who is modeled on Murrell), escapes, forming a link with the next tale in the series. Richard's own story ends, foreseeably, with his return to the arms of Mary.

Simms's immediate purpose in spinning the sensational story of *Richard Hurdis* was the hope of titillating a large body of readers. But if it is read attentively a secondary intention emerges: Simms wished to examine more deeply than he had in *Guy Rivers* the nature of the primitive frontier inhabitants.

A haunting question underlies the highly colored incidents of the plot: What is the meaning of this border violence and outlawry? If the border could produce a man like Thumbscrew Witherspoon, why did it also spawn a gang dedicated only to acts against organized society?

Simms offers an answer in an episode in which Richard, bound for exile, meets a band of emigrants from North Carolina. His first impression is one of sympathy for these "Mississippi mad" pioneers—a "simple and hardy people, looking poor, but proud" (66)—who are bound west in wagons crammed with all their possessions. But reflection leads Richard to a melancholy conclusion as he thinks of the "deserted country" they have left and the reasons behind their trek into the vacant West. For it is hope of easy wealth and not the establishment of community that is driving them onward. They are itching to despoil the land, not to make it theirs and to become a part of it. It is this wastefulness, this moving on to new regions when former ones have been exploited, that Simms deplores: "The wandering habits of our people are the great obstacle to their perfect civilization. These habits are encouraged by the cheapness of our public lands. and their constant exposure for sale." The result of this policy, in Simms's mind, had been a lowering of personal morality and the consequent breakdown of the structure of communal living: "The morals not less than the manners of our people are diseased by the license of the wilderness; and the remoteness of the white settler from his former associates approximate him to the savage feebleness of the Indian . . ." (66).[8]

Simms's social concern thus gives a broader dimension to the sensational tale of blood that *Richard Hurdis* relates. At the beginning of the story Richard is at fault because for personal reasons he is ready to reject the security which has resulted from his ancestors' having carved a plantation (part of an ordered world) out of the wilds. By his self-imposed exile he is in effect becoming a traitor; he is selling out a decent society which can grow only if such young men as he accept the past and insure its continuity. It is revealing that Simms has Richard redeem himself: as the tale ends, he has been cleansed of his false views by direct experience of a disordered world; and he returns to marry his Mary and to settle into the planter's life. Like Mellichampe, he has been brought by trials back to essential nobility.

The robber band has a similar thematic function. Its guilt is not simply that the members are outlaws; by banding together they have substituted for honorable society a corrupted "brotherhood." In the scenes in which Richard becomes an initiate, Simms gives this idea melodramatic development. The band's degrees of rank, its bravery, its group loyalty, its unquestioning acceptance of authority are all parodies of authentic values, because they are dedicated to selfish ends. Like the North Carolina emigrants, the outlaws have immediacy as their motto and material wealth as their goal. Again it is significant that Simms makes the planter class—Colonel Grafton and Richard— the agents for shattering the domination of the lawless.

Simms's view of border society as it is expressed in *Richard Hurdis* comes to this: The new lands can have real value only when the borderers are ready to develop them with the future of man in mind. The land must not be wasted or despoiled—or society will die along with it. That is why the scout, who is in harmony with the wild, is a "natural noble" to Simms; that is why the self-seeking outlaw, the wanderer, and the squatter are types who must fall before the carriers of civilization. *Richard Hurdis* has all of Simms's common flaws. But, almost intuitively, he touched upon a theme—the fate of the virgin wilderness—which has remained a powerful one in American writing. And by relating it to his objective of a structured society, he achieved what was, in many ways, the most significantly Southern romance he had yet composed.

III *The Actor and the Outlaws*

Apparently yearning to prove he could produce a successful foreign romance, Simms delayed a while the obvious sequel to *Richard Hurdis* (Foster, the bandit leader, is still at large and must be brought to book). What he next hastily published was another richly costumed but fundamentally sham pageant of the past, *The Damsel of Darien* (1839), a depiction of Balboa in Spanish America. The effort revealed that he had learned nothing from the writing of *Pelayo*. It was not simply a question of subject matter, for tales of Spain had delighted the public;

recent examples were Washington Irving's *The Alhambra* (1832) and Robert Montgomery Bird's *Calavar* (1834). But Simms entirely lacked the knack of giving life to a scene about which he knew nothing, and the *Damsel* fully merited the scolding which Lawson gave it in a New York journal.[9] Simms was to dig into the history of other nations only twice more—in *Count Julian* (1845), the sequel to *Pelayo;* and in *Vasconselos* (1853). Then he was, happily for his readers, resigned to leaving the field to others more competent than he.

In his review Lawson had cuttingly but truthfully pointed out that Simms wrote so much and published so often that it was not surprising that he should founder now and then. The justice of his remark was again embarrassingly displayed in Simms's next long work of fiction, *Border Beagles* (1840), which he called "A Tale of Mississippi." Merely as a sequel to *Richard Hurdis* it fails to recapture the excitement generated by that book, and the new elements which he introduced exposed a wavering intention.

In this third border romance Simms should have gone on directly with the pursuit of the bandit Foster and tied up the loose ends. The outlaw's capture is accomplished in *Border Beagles,* but by the story's close Foster has been so lost in the welter of plot and counterplot that the reader has long since ceased to care what happens to him. Moreover, his eventual nemesis, Harry Vernon (who takes the place and most of the characteristics of Richard Hurdis), has no real drive to track him down, though he holds the governor's commission to do so. Vernon has his own quest: to locate the man who had cheated an older friend of money and sweetheart; and this complication edges the taking of the villain into a subordinate position. In *Richard Hurdis* Foster, the not unintelligent exponent of outlawry, had been an interesting creation, one of Simms's most believable knaves; in *Border Beagles,* given the new name of Saxon and placed in a subplot involving his lust for Vernon's girl friend, he changes into a literary posturer of the Guy Rivers ilk. And with the loss of his earlier personality goes the reader's interest in his fate.

Even more fundamental a factor undermining the story is the constant intrusion of Simms's fascination with the theater. Much of the book is devoted to the picaresque adventures of one Tom Horsey, a young Mississippian who has acted with stock companies throughout the South. Horsey is created in the worst "humour" vein; his ruling passion is the stage, and he constantly interlards his fantastical conversation with scraps from the old English dramatists. The details of the actor's life, which are sometimes diverting, are probably drawn from Simms's own observations. But Horsey, intended as a comic figure, lacks a genuine sense of humor himself and carries on like a dimwit. He can even live for a while among an outlaw band under the impression that they are itinerant actors preparing for a tour!

Simms possibly felt that he was placating those carpers who had found *Richard Hurdis* "too stern, gloomy and even savage of character" (he snarls back at them in his foreword). But in going to the other extreme and subordinating the theme of frontier violence to an interest in the character of Horsey, he came up with something far worse—a comedy that falls flat. This was no "tale of Mississippi" at all, but a tired reworking of parts of *Richard Hurdis* hashed up with something he thought entirely novel. These last two years had been a period of faltering—of seeking new subjects and a new audience. Simms would stumble again, but at least in his next book (another Revolutionary romance) he was back on home territory amid the scenes which he always handled most convincingly.

CHAPTER 6

Black Riders

I *Supple Jack*

SIMMS ADDED one more installment to his continuing narrative of the American Revolution with *The Scout* (1841).
But he was still in the mood which had given birth to the
recent border romances, and he now fabricated a tale which
suggests a transplanting of *Richard Hurdis* to the 1780's. As in
Mellichampe, he concentrated not on any grand strategy but
rather on one of the private quarrels intermingled with the
campaigns; and, with no overall concern with lofty historical
events, he fell back upon devices that were becoming con-
spicuously creaky.

The central subject of *The Scout,* like that of *Richard Hurdis,*
is the conflict between two brothers—one warm, impetuous,
and honorable; the other cold, crafty, and egocentric. Clarence
Conway, like Singleton, is a partisan leader whose abilities match
those of that earlier worthy; Edward, his half-brother, secretly
heads the Tory "Black Riders," a band of marauding roughnecks
who take orders from the British when not off on their own.
Both kinsmen are in love with Flora Middleton, a patriotic miss
from Katharine Walton's mold. After due soul-searching about
being forced to fight his father's son, Clarence at last emerges
the expected victor and gains the noble if somewhat chilly
Flora. Edward, who is dogged throughout the tale by a young
country woman whom he has seduced, naturally comes to the
ignominious end that this evidence of his lust demands. In the
meantime, there are captivities, unexpected rescues, misunder-
standings between the lovers, a liberal amount of stagy turbulence
(including a sensationally overwrought duel between the brothers

in the Middleton family tomb), and much venting of high-flown sentiment about the Carolinians' cause.

As this stark summary indicates, *The Scout* wears trappings calculated to fetch a popular audience; and if it offered nothing more it could hardly stand serious dissection. But once again Simms did much to redeem his story by bringing in a new back-woods scout called "Supple Jack" Bannister. Like his predecessors, Bannister acts as a cooling influence upon Clarence Conway and as the spokesman for middle-class virtue and solidity of character. But more than they he is also the average Southerner repulsing foreign tyranny; Bannister knows why he is fighting and is concerned that others understand his reasons.

In one well-written scene Simms gives the stage entirely to the scout. Bannister has run across an old acquaintance who chose the Tory side, and he attempts to "convert" him—first by words, then by a physical thrashing. The latter argument is the more convincing to the Tory himself, but Bannister's long plea for the patriots' cause sounds the romance's serious theme. Recalling one occasion when he had killed a British officer with whom the Tory was traveling, the scout muses on the meaning of the incident to him:

> "I wasn't sorry that I killed him, and I would shoot the very next one that came along, jest the same; for it made the gall bile up in me to see a man that I had never said a hard word to in all my life, come here, over the water, a matter, maybe, of a thousand miles, to force me, at the p'int of the bagnet, to drink stamped tea. I never did drink the tea, no how. . . . But, 'twas the freedom of the thing that I was argying for, and 'twas on the same argyment that I was willing to fight. . . .
>
> "Well, it so happens that I won't pay George the Third any more taxes. That's the word for all; and it's good reason why I shouldn't pay him, when, for all his trying, he can't make me. Here he's sent his rigiments—rigiment after rigiment—and the queen sent her rigiment, and the prince of Wales his rigiment—I reckon we didn't tear the prince's rigiment all to flinders at Hanging Rock!—Well, then, there was the Royal Scotch and the Royal Irish, and the Dutch Hessians;—I suppose they didn't call them royal, 'cause they couldn't ax in English for what they wanted:—well, what was the good of it?—all these rigiments together, couldn't make poor Jack Bannister, a Congaree boatman, drink stamped tea or pay taxes. The rigiments, all I've named,

and a hundred more, are gone like last autumn's dry leaves; and the only fighting that's a-going on now, worth to speak of, is American born 'gainst American born. . . ."[1]

This is the authentic voice of the liberty-loving frontiersman, and Simms reproduces its accents deftly. It is, we may say, far more realistic in its present effect than are the rhetorical flourishes which mark the similar speeches of the heroes and heroines. But both classes were genuine to Simms, and each speaks in a manner he believed to be appropriate. Both types, shown here in their formative stages during the Revolution, are the forerunners of those Southerners who would defend their cause in another war yet to come. Of the inevitability of this future conflict of brother against brother—of "American born 'gainst American born"—Simms could not have been conscious in 1841. But in the four Revolutionary romances that remained to be written he tended more and more to draw a parallel between the patriotic side in the War of Independence and the attitude of his state in the decade just prior to the Civil War.

Ten years were to elapse now before he began the drive to complete his imaginative recasting of the Revolution, and by 1851 armed strife between North and South appeared to him a probability. Not surprisingly, it was in the 1850's that the legend of the invincible South, which he had been developing for twenty years, received its fullest expression.

II *The Blind Heart*

The Scout had been published early in 1841. In March of that year Simms mentioned to Lawson that he was turning over in his mind the material for a new tale, "the scene of which will lie partly in my native city" (*L*, I, 236). Just five months later he announced that the book was finished, and it soon appeared as *Confession; or, The Blind Heart*.

Simms supplied a partial explanation for this incredibly rapid composition in some introductory remarks to the story. He had recently been "exploring the contents of a large mass" of manuscripts dating from his early years and had come across a fragment which "possessed his mind so warmly" that he "could not resist the desire to resume it." Then, he continued, while he was attempting to arrange it for the press, "the work grew beneath his hands to a size far exceeding his original purpose."[2] As the student of Simms comes to know, such rediscovery of old and usable material generally set the author's pen to scrambling but left his creative imagination idling. *Confession*, one of the longest works in the canon, is no exception.

Simms was to concede later that the basic idea of the book was "a dangerous one" (*L*, I, 278). It was indeed; he tried to outdo Shakespeare's *Othello* by offering a protagonist whose jealousy arose only from his own misinterpretation of scenes he had witnessed—that is, he had no Iago operating upon him. The story expanded itself into a "psychological novel"; and like all of Simms's other struggles to compose in the contemporary, domestic vein, it is the stillborn child of dogged determination alone.

The plot is worth a brief review since it so perfectly exposes why Simms failed in the genre of the novel as he had defined it in the *Yemassee* preface. Edward Clifford, a rising young lawyer in the town of C——(presumably Charleston), has wed the beautiful Julia, whose artistic interests he unfortunately cannot entirely share. Into this household vacuum is drawn William Edgerton, who is patently lured by something more than Julia's drawing skill; and Clifford's fatal jealousy is at once excited. To avoid the triangle he now sees forming, Clifford takes Julia to Alabama; but Edgerton reappears on a visit for "his health." Goaded by what he takes to be evidences of his wife's infidelity, Clifford challenges Edgerton to a duel. With the time and place set, Clifford, expecting to kill Edgerton, poisons his wife and goes off to meet his rival. But Edgerton has forestalled him by committing suicide after he has left a note confessing that any guilt was his alone. Still not convinced of his wife's fidelity, Clifford returns to his office and discovers a letter from Julia, sent the previous day, which so corroborates Edgerton's account that he at last realizes that he has been duped by his "blind heart." Told by a friend that he deserves the punishment of remaining alive, Clifford sets off for Texas to seek atonement for his stupidity.

Like Simms's first short novel *Martin Faber*, *Confession* falters just where it needs to succeed—in believable motivation. The reader is left wondering: Why did Julia not simply tell her husband the details which she informed him of by letter? Why did Clifford not earlier confront either Julia or Edgerton with his suspicions? Clifford, as Simms renders him, is not an understandably jealous man but a novelistic contrivance; and, with our realization of this fact, the whole ponderous structure collapses. It is not a tragedy of character, because Clifford has none; the protagonist is an automaton wound up and set to walking a straight course to the brink. It is theatricality without being drama.

Into this pseudo-*Othello*, Simms inserts one curious and jarring incident which indicates that, even when he was ostensibly avoiding the themes he had developed in the border and Revolutionary romances, his concern with the South could still intrude. This is a scene in which a friend of Clifford makes a half-jesting, half-serious prediction of political upheaval. He feels that an American conquest of Canada is inevitable and that the South will suffer because the new territory will be "New England all over." The South, therefore, must also scheme; Texas should continue to be settled with thousands of dependable Southerners and when the region is powerful enough Mexico can be seized. Cuba and other West Indian isles are to follow in this timetable of Southern expansionism, and one day there will be a new empire: "a great and glorious country—stretching from the gulf to the Pacific, and providing the natural balance, which, in a few years, the southern states of this Union will inevitably need" (Chapter XXVIII).

This passage need not be taken too literally, since it is expressed in a hyperbolic spirit. Yet it clearly bares Simms's growing conviction that the South had to seek a balance of power if it was to protect its institutions. As we know, this doctrine of Southern nationhood was to expand into a truly deadly course of action. But as an idea it was relevant to Simms's whole myth of the South; and, when we ponder how he might have developed a hint that he only casually dropped into this puppet-play of the passions, we may regret that for the time being he had decided to be a novelist.

III *The Kentucky Tragedy*

The basic faults of *Confession* were further compounded in Simms's next work of fiction, *Beauchampe*, which followed just a year later (1842). *Beauchampe* is often classed as a border romance, and it does deal with the sort of dark emotions and sensationalism that had characterized the other frontier tales. But Simms's main concern again was in probing the inner motivations of his major players, and there is little organic rendering of the Southern background.

The immediate source of *Beauchampe* was a notorious murder case of the 1820's—one that has passed into literature as "the Kentucky tragedy."[3] In his tale Simms constructs the general outlines as the public had come to know them: Warham Sharpe, a prominent attorney, seduces Margaret Cooper, who vows to kill him after he deserts her. Margaret finds her chance when she accepts the proposal of a young law student, Beauchampe, for he, after hearing her story, is willing to be the agent of her vengeance. When Sharpe refuses to duel and makes slurring remarks about Margaret, Beauchampe in fury slays him, is put on trial, and condemned. Shortly before his scheduled execution he and Margaret stab themselves in his cell and she dies at once. But Beauchampe's wounds do not prove fatal until he is on the way to the gallows, and he manages to cry out to the crowd that at least the women of Kentucky will bless his name for having acted for Margaret's honor.

The facts behind the real-life case were confused enough, and it matters little whether Simms was striving for accuracy in his own retelling. For his story fails simply as story. The main characters are analyzed incessantly but unconvincingly, and they are too simply conceived to bear the implications of the plot itself. Here was a ready-made instance of savagery suddenly springing out of Southern society, involving overtones of border politics, of chicanery in office, of immorality hiding behind the mask of respectability—and Simms failed to come to grips with these complexities. He was unable to relate these real, bloody events to the kind of civilization he had described in other works; he could not shape the factual materials into anything of his own.

Fundamentally, this is the reason all Simms's psychological novels miscarry and why the Revolutionary romances are more often successful. In his novels he was too close to surface minutiae, too insistent that he had his details correct to be able to see that they lacked the one element that could make them right: imaginative recasting into the artificial world of fiction. In the Revolutionary tales, on the other hand, he had begun with a general theme—the war as a heroic period that had helped to mold the Southern character—and he had unfolded it through representative or symbolic types. Whether or not he sensed this truth, he was to make a literary recovery only when he returned to this theme—some nine years later.

IV Periodicals and Politics

In the interval between *Beauchampe* (1842) and *Katharine Walton* (1851), Simms produced only a few scattered new, long works of fiction. At first consideration the fact is astonishing, for in a publishing career of about seventeen years he had brought out fourteen separate romances, novels, and collections of short tales. There had also been several volumes of poetry and other miscellaneous books—more than twenty in all. This interim period shows no diminution of his literary labors, for he bettered his mark in terms of total productivity. Yet nonfiction and poetry far outweigh the volumes of fiction, and none of the latter shows an advance over the best of his earlier prose.

As amply evidenced by Simms's letters between 1842 and 1851, two chief factors influenced his turning away from the long romance: financial necessity, which drove him into editorial posts, and increasing concern with immediate political affairs. The first motive was particularly nagging. His romances, which had on the whole been welcomed by press and reading public, were not now enticing as much cash as he needed. Competition from newer writers, and higher publishing costs meant a corresponding reduction in his sales; and he—unlike Cooper—was not able to have stereotype plates made against the hope of future demand. Meanwhile, life at "Woodlands" was not the happy time on the old plantation that some postwar writers would dream of. He was encumbered by debt, constantly subjected to losses in bad agricultural years, and burdened by the demands of a rapidly growing family. Obviously he had to try all possible outlets for his writing skills.

In the marketing of material Simms was a giant in these years. Yet all his pages are little more than hack work born of immediate pressure; not one production in any of the varied fields to which he now turned opened up an area comparable to the beginning he had made in creating a native Southern fiction. No more than a list is required to indicate the extent of Simms's efforts in this active but comparatively fruitless time. There were nine volumes of poetry, most of them collections of previously printed verses; six works of fiction, including *Count Julian* (which had been written some years earlier), *Helen Halsey* (a border tale), and *The Wigwam and the Cabin* (a gathering of short stories);[4] four biographies—of Francis Marion, Captain John Smith, the Chevalier Bayard, and Nathanael Greene; a volume about the early history of Florida; two volumes devoted to the geography of South Carolina; an edition of the Shakespeare apochrypha; several orations; and two volumes of literary criticism, *Views and Reviews*, which contain a plea for Americanism in literature and an essay of homage to Cooper.

In addition to producing these books, Simms contributed regularly to several journals and, at intervals, acted as an editor.[5] One magazine, *The Magnolia*, was even moved to Charleston to enable Simms to take over its management. Its prospectus, issued in 1842, is so typical of the ambitious aims of these Southern literary men that it must be quoted. Said its publisher, P. C. Pendleton:

> We rejoice to believe that the day of Southern lukewarmness to the necessity of mental culture, in our own land, has gone by forever. There is a glorious awakening. We have daily signs that a Southern literature is demanded. . . . We are proud in detecting, in the progress of each day's events, the decisive proofs that our people need, and are determined to have, a periodical, which shall speak justly and fear not;—which shall be equally true and bold; in which criticism shall be free from cant, and opinion shall be unbiassed either by fear or favor;—a work in which the tone shall be manly, and the character and sentiment essentially and only Southern. . . . We feel the sentiment of Southern intellectual independence, every where, beginning to breath[e] and burn around us. . . . [The document is reproduced in *L*, I, facing p. 329.]

Unfortunately these warm apostles of a Southern literature were never so well endowed with cash as they were with a heady prose style, and the *Magnolia* soon drooped and died. More effectual was the *Southern and Western Magazine and Review* to which Simms's contributions (under several signatures) were so regular that it was popularly known as "Simms's

Magazine"; it was merged in 1846 with the Richmond *Southern Literary Messenger,* which had counted Simms as an old friend and which, under the editorship of Poe, reached a high position among Southern periodicals. Three years after this merger Simms took over the recently founded *Southern Quarterly Review,* and he wrestled with its problems until late 1854.

Even a cursory glance through a bound volume of any of these journals gives one a notion of the taste of the times—and also of the frustrations that plagued a serious professional writer. In general, the publications, in bondage to romantic and sentimental fashions, avoided experimentation. Their poetry sections were crammed with steamy love lyrics, elegiac verse, and long narrative poems in the manner of Scott and Byron. The fiction department was always good for a few short emotional tales (occasionally on native themes) and serializations of overblown novels. A serious balance was sometimes attempted with scholarly articles on classical literature, politics, and foreign travel—all of which gave Southern lawyers, clergymen, teachers, and gentlemen in any situation the chance to display their learning in a properly nonprofessional way. The editorial or critical division was the burden of the editor (or editors), and in it many competent craftsmen wasted time and bile in belaboring the output of the popular press. In all these departments Simms toiled wearyingly and unprofitably; frequently his own contributions came close to filling the major portion of an issue. It is no wonder that one of the favorite phrases in his correspondence became "brain sweat."

The second factor, in addition to his editorial career, that helped keep Simms away from long fiction during this decade was his involvement in politics. He had from his earliest years been concerned with Southern government; now, as outside pressures became more sharp, he went directly into the arena. Just after 1840 his friendship with James Henry Hammond became an especially vital influence on his public activities. Hammond had been a member of Congress and was governor of South Carolina from 1842 to 1844; he was to be a United States senator during the critical period just before the Civil War. But a personal scandal had set back his higher ambitions, and he was forced for a time to lead a retired life on a plantation not far distant from Simms's. The minds of the two men were closely attuned in social and political matters, if not always in literary judgments: Hammond could be a severe critic of Simms's tales. Both were tireless advocates of Southern institutions; both favored expansionism for the South; both felt that the strength of John C. Calhoun had necessarily reduced the stature of other South Carolina politicians; and both hoped for a day when Hammond could again become a force on the national stage.

The long series of letters between the two men, which began in the 1840's, is a fascinating running commentary on the issues which were relentlessly driving the South toward open war. Confidential and even conspiratorial in tone, they frankly discuss the irreconcilable differences between North and South and debate means for strengthening the South's internal ties. Simms was to say of Hammond after his death: "We had few or no secrets from each other—we took few steps in life without mutual consultation. . . . I felt that there was something akin in our intellectual nature" (*L*, IV, 469). But it must be added that the influence of Hammond the politician on Simms the literary man was not for the best. For Hammond helped to stimulate in Simms a yearning for similar involvement; and the enormous energies (eventually futile) which Simms put into seeking public advancement necessarily undercut his serious writing. Simms was elected to the state legislature in 1844, but the next year he lost the race to become lieutenant-governor. Like other American writers—Irving and Hawthorne, for example—he also pulled strings for a diplomatic post abroad; but unlike them, he failed to win one. After this final effort at recognition, Simms retired from active politics, although he never entirely ceased working behind the scenes.

The whole experience of this decade was an upsetting one. Steady disappointments—political, familial, financial, and literary—had taken their physical and emotional toll; and it was a disillusioned Simms who poured out his troubles in a long letter to Hammond at the close of 1847. For its survey of his career to date and for its despondent forecast of his prospects, it warrants quoting at some length:

> I am greatly behind hand with my publishers. I have numerous tasks before me which I cannot neglect. On the performance of these tasks depend my resources, which, to deal with you frankly, are small & diminishing. My residence in South Carolina, is

unfavorable to me as an author. I lose $2000 per annum by it. Our planting interests barely pay expenses and my income from Literature which in 1835 was $6000 per annum, is scarce $1500 now, owing to the operation of cheap reprints which pay publishers & printers profits only & yield the author little or nothing. To earn this $1500 I have to labor constantly, and being absent from the field, I labor at a venture, not being able to seize upon the occasion. I think, accordingly, to remove from the State to New York. . . . Here I am nothing & can be & do nothing. The South don't care a d--n for literature or art. Your best neighbour & kindred never think to buy books. They will borrow from you & beg, but the same man who will always have his wine, has no idea of a library. You will write for & defend their institutions in vain. They will not pay the expense of printing your essays. . . . At the North, the usual gift to a young lady is a book—in the South, a ring, a chain, or a bottle of Eau de Cologne! [*L*, II, 385-86].

If this mood of bitterness had lasted, Simms might well have gone North, as he considered doing; and his career could have taken a new direction under the influence of his many literary acquaintances there. But the pull of the South was too strong upon him, and it was upon his own soil that he made both a professional and personal recovery after 1851. It was more than just a tested subject that made him return to Revolutionary days in several of the best tales he ever composed; it was, in a sense, a call not to be denied. For in the 1850's the South increasingly felt beleaguered, and it was subject to attacks by hostile outside forces as it had been in the late eighteenth century. To many, it had been sold out by the country for which it had once so nobly fought. More and more deeply Simms was to make an emotional connection between the two epochs. And so it was that in these historical romances his creative powers and his devotion to the cause of the South could now again be most effectively joined.

CHAPTER 7

The Road Back

I *Loyalties*

KATHARINE WALTON (1851) shows an altered attitude toward the subjects which Simms had introduced in the first three of the Revolutionary romances. Though returning to the usual skirmishes between partisans and British troops, it puts more emphasis upon character than upon thrilling action; and it tries to illustrate the civilized emotions of the combatants. It thus loses some of the exuberance and headlong pace of the earlier stories, but it also gains in its balanced presentation of the several sides in the conflict. It is not so well integrated as the three remaining tales about the war which Simms was to write next; too much of the book is given over to tiresome affairs of high society in the garrison city of Charleston. But it brought Simms again before the public with the topic that he had made specifically his own, and it stimulated him to continue with the most inspired writing of his career.

In terms of plot, *Katharine Walton* looks back to the first of the series, *The Partisan.* Old Colonel Walton, the wealthy land-owner who had taken the king's protection and who had then been converted by Singleton, is out on foraying expeditions, leaving his daughter Katharine and her old aunt on the family plantation. But Walton's rebellion has rendered his lands subject to British confiscation, and the plunderers now swoop down. Eager to have the estate for himself, the British commandant Balfour insists that the proud Katharine and her aunt move into Charleston as virtual prisoners; and the central portion of the story is given over to the life of Briton, loyalist, and rebel in the occupied town. Simms informs us regularly that he has drawn from history and tradition in order to create a faithful portrait of real people, but what he produced was a dreary imitation of the eighteenth-century drama and the novel of manners. There are soirées, love games, epigram-spouting fops, duels—even a runaway marriage. But luckily the war intrudes—and Simms surprisingly manages a twist on an old plot device. Colonel Walton is again captured, but this time Singleton and his band do not sweep out of the swamps to rescue him. He is hanged after a tearful farewell scene with Katharine; and the tale ends rather abruptly with Simms's reassurance to his readers that Katharine experienced happier days after her marriage with Singleton.

Reduced to this summary, *Katharine Walton* would appear to have contributed little to Simms's concept of a developing Southern order. But the book's constantly reiterated theme is loyalty to the land and the vital role which that loyalty has played in changing the tide of the war. The motif is carried particularly through the story of General Williamson, an American officer who had laid down his arms after early defeats and had conceded victory to the British. Caught by Colonel Walton and charged with his defection, Williamson tries to excuse himself by recalling that Walton, too, had once been ready to compromise. Walton flushes at the memory and can retort only that *he* is not the one now on trial. Williamson's reply is remarkable for its attempted defense of those who had been willing to surrender to save themselves and their homes from destruction:

"In referring to the protection taken by yourself, I meant only to indicate the true character of that compromise which the necessities of the time forced so many of us to make. Until Buford's defeat, I appeal to all the world to say, if I did not honorably and truly maintain my allegiance to the revolutionary party. But in the defeat of Buford went down all organized opposition in the state. It was supposed, on all hands, that the contest was at an end, so far as South Carolina and Georgia were concerned."[1]

But Williamson's appeal to expediency—like that of Walton himself in *The Partisan*—is not to be accepted, though he is allowed his say. Both officers—men high in the leader class—have faltered in their loyalty to their native soil, and both must suffer the penalty for wavering. This is the reason Simms allows Walton to go to the gallows; though he has partially atoned by his recent aid to the partisans, he can fully redeem himself only by gallantly meeting death at the hands of those to whom he once submitted.

A more unexpected treatment of the dilemmas of loyalty comes through the character of a British officer—the Major Proctor who had fallen in love with Katharine Walton and who had been notably snubbed by her in *The Partisan*. Proctor has been forced out of his command by a cabal of fellow officers, and his sense of personal injustice has opened his mind to the possibility that the Americans may after all have some virtue on their side. In a talk with Singleton (who for the time being is in disguise as a British sympathizer in order to spy upon the enemy), he confesses that England has erred in trying to force obedience to the mother country:

"The true loyalty is to the soil, or rather to the race. I am persuaded that one is never more safe in his principles than when he takes side with his kindred. There is a virtue in the race which strengthens and secures our own; and he is never more in danger of proving in the wrong than when he resolutely opposes himself to the sentiments of his people. At all events, one may reasonably distrust the virtue in his principle when he finds himself called upon to sustain it by actually drawing his sword against his kindred" (126).

These have been precisely Singleton's own sentiments, and a bond of close friendship grows between the quondam enemies. For Proctor has been a professional soldier merely assigned to a task; he has become disillusioned by the petty intrigues and by the lust for personal gain which have cost him his position, and he is driven so far from his past that he ultimately marries an American and settles down in the South against which he had fought.

This repeated mention of loyalty to one's own soil is a measure of how intensely Simms was coming to identify his Revolutionary patriots with rebellious South Carolinians of the 1850's; once again his state should stand against all tyranny from without. His preface to *Katharine Walton* specifically announces his awareness of the example of the past. With "a natural feeling of pride and satisfaction," he gazed back over what he had already done for Southern fiction:

> I may be permitted to say that they [the Revolutionary romances] were, when originally published, so many new developments and discoveries to our people. They opened the way to historical studies among us—they suggested clews to the historian—they struck and laid bare to other workers, the veins of tradition which everywhere enriched our territory—they showed to succeeding laborers—far abler than myself—what treasures of *materiel*, lay waiting for the shaping hands of future genius. When I first began these fictions, no one dreamed of the abundance of our possessions of this sort—that a scene or story, picture or statue, had been wrought out of the crude masses which lay buried in our soil. My friends denounced my waste of time upon scenes, and situations, and events, in which they beheld nothing latent—nothing which could possibly (as they thought) reward the laborer. *Now*, South Carolina is regarded as a very storehouse for romance. She has furnished more materials for the use of art and fiction, than half the states in the Union . . . [3].

It was with this renewed sense of his past achievements—of his discovery of a vitally useful "myth of the South"—that Simms undertook the three works which form the most carefully wrought segment of the Revolutionary romances.

II *Soldier's Pay*

The national Compromise of 1850, whereby the South won a new and stringent fugitive-slave law but lost a large amount of Western territory to the anti-slavery forces, brought a brief period of relief to many worried Southerners. But in South Carolina, not for nothing dubbed the "Hotspur state," the spirit of compromise was notably lacking. Both in the Southern convention held in Nashville in June, 1850, and in the state's own similar meeting two years later, many of its citizens exhibited the adamancy which was to put it in the van of the secession movement. Grown reckless in springing up to defend their institutions, Carolinians were retorting to the North in words and actions challenging enough to alarm even some of their Southern neighbors. Their mood was certainly not improved by the appearance in 1852 of Harriet Beecher Stowe's sensational portrayal of slavery in *Uncle Tom's Cabin.*

During this simmering period Simms was playing an active but behind-the-scenes role. In frequent letters to his favorite political correspondents, James Henry Hammond and Beverley Tucker, he bitterly castigated other Southern states for their timidity and urged active support for South Carolina's leadership. A formal split, he now felt, was inevitable; the only real problem was to be the selection of the proper moment and the method. Writing to Tucker in March, 1851, he firmly took his stand: "We are all anxious to relieve ourselves from the existing national incubus, and the question is one purely of time. My own notion is that the Union, even if we remain quiescent, cannot last five years. Abolition, which is not a placable madness —not to be soothed—if let alone will so kick your state [Virginia] & others, that resistance becomes inevitable . . ." (*L*, III, 99).

What Simms calls the "madness" of the abolition movement was to sweep large sections of the nation just a year later when *Uncle Tom's Cabin* started on its meteoric rise to fame. Simms, as the leading Southern literary exponent of the slave system, could hardly fail to strike back at Mrs. Stowe; but the method he chose was somewhat unexpected. He did not himself review the book in the *Southern Quarterly Review,* which he was then editing, and he did not discuss it fully in print until Mrs. Stowe published *A Key to Uncle Tom's Cabin* some time later.[2] Instead, he chose the positive course of presenting in a work of fiction an extended account of what he conceived the whole Southern system ideally to be. This new book was *Woodcraft,* the fifth of the Revolutionary romances.

There can be no doubt that this reply to *Uncle Tom's Cabin* was Simms's own design, for he commented in a letter to Hammond that his latest romance was "probably as good an answer to Mrs. Stowe as has been published" (*L*, III, 222-23). And that Hammond accepted it as such is clear from his remark: "On the whole I think it fully equal to any of your novels, & that you have admirably defended our 'Institution' & elevated it in some respects" (*L*, III, 243, n. 64). But *Woodcraft* is not at all what one might anticipate from these statements. Comparatively mild in tone, sharp in characterization, occasionally farcical, it may at a casual reading seem unrelated to any immediate tensions. However, Simms's main themes are clearly expressed, and as a whole the book is stronger for making its points without appearing to insist upon them.

Simms was faced with at least a double problem as he began its composition. In the first place, there was his wide readership. He did have to consider that much of his income depended upon Northern readers; too blatant a defense (like the pointedly anti-Tom books that were appearing) could only bring alienation. Secondly, since he held—as his review of the *Key* and some other statements make evident—that Mrs. Stowe's slaveowners were in no way representative, he could not admit and thus respond to her scenes of horror and of weeping sentimentality about the slaves' lot. The *Key* review attacked the probability of the characters, situations, and events in *Uncle Tom's Cabin;* though any one of these might be possible in isolation, none ought to be taken as basis for generalization about the Southern way of life. Character and event in his own story had to carry the conviction that here was truth as recorded by a person within the system—not the wrongheaded views of a Northern outsider who, as the *Key* itself explained, had based her novel on material which she had been forced to dig up. Tone, moreover, had to be carefully controlled. Mrs. Stowe had made her appeal to the heart by way of the tear ducts, and her book evoked a passionate resentment against all who were connected with slavery. Simms's handling of this touchy problem of tone is perhaps the main technical achievement of his story. He had to create in his own readers a mood of tacit acceptance of the scene as presented; he had to avoid directly stirring up sectional bias. The method he chose, therefore, was humor. Though the long book does have subplots and moments of terror, it is fundamentally the story of one person—that true son of the Old South, Porgy. And it is the rotund Porgy's unflagging wit and good nature that set the tale's major mood.

Although *Woodcraft* is the fifth in order of appearance of the seven Revolutionary romances, it is in terms of the chronology of the war the final chapter. As the story opens, the defeated British are evacuating Charleston and are trying to salvage as much plunder as possible. The chief booty, significantly, is slaves, whom the enemy have been stealing and shipping secretly to the West Indies. Widow Eveleigh, an old friend and

neighbor of Porgy's, is aware of this dirty dealing; in a confronta-
tion with the British commander she is able to prove that a
scheduled shipment contains some of her own and of Porgy's
Negroes. She forces their release; but the Tory M'Kewn, who
had supplied the slaves, and his crony Bostwick, a squatter on
lands near Porgy's plantation, are determined not to let their
reward money slip away. They plot an attack on the Widow's
party as she returns to her home in the backlands.

Simms now weaves in the second strand of this first segment
of the book. Porgy is on the road back to his war-ruined house
with a few ragged followers: his lieutenant, young Lance
Frampton; his aide, blunt, one-armed Sergeant Millhouse; and
his devoted slave Tom. There is a momentary vein of bitterness
as Simms takes up, on perhaps the first occasion in American
fiction, the now familiar theme of "soldier's pay."[3] For the
partisans have learned that because of their appearance and
condition they have been denied the fun of watching the de-
parture of the British troops, and they are properly disgusted:

> But [their indignation] did not declare itself, and could not,
> while under the leaders who had so nobly conducted them
> throughout the war; and now they were to be disbanded—to
> separate from their leaders—to pay the last honors of salute to
> the colors they had so often watched in the heady storms and
> vicissitudes of battle, and to retire to their homes—such homes
> as a war of seven years had left them—homes in ruins;—and
> to sink unhonored into an obscurity which held forth little
> promise of distinction in the future, and still less of improving
> fortunes [48].

But this is a story of postwar courage and not of disillusionment, and the dark mood is quickly dispelled as Porgy and
his followers ride in upon the attempt by M'Kewn's men to
hold up Widow Eveleigh. The skirmishing and bloodshed which
follow take us back to the spirit of the earlier romances; Simms
was willing thus far to live up to his readers' expectations.
Finally the Widow and her retinue are rescued; she, observing
the poverty of the partisans, insists upon giving them some of
the immediate necessities for their homecoming.

The return home forms the second main section of *Woodcraft*,
and Simms skillfully paints the dismal scene. The plantation

house is stripped, the fields are choked with weeds, and all livestock has vanished. Only the few slaves whom the Widow has saved from deportation remain to join in the task of rebuilding. It is crucial to note how Simms has thus far handled the two elements which make up the first half of the book—the road back and the homecoming. He has insinuated details of slavery and of the Southern social order from the opening pages on, but he has subordinated them to scenes of exciting action. Having now, hopefully, captured his readers' interest, Simms could turn to developing the subject that makes up the rest of the story: restoration of the plantation way of life.

With the exception of a subplot involving a growing feud between the two villains, M'Kewn and Bostwick, the tale is now largely confined to Porgy's home and environs. Porgy knows that M'Kewn has long held a mortgage on his property, and he anticipates that the Tory will soon demand his debt. Sergeant Millhouse, though, sees a way to resolve this quandary: Porgy must marry the rich Widow Eveleigh. Simms squeezes some merriment out of Porgy's comic wooing, but he allows his hero no success. And so when the sheriff arrives with the expected eviction order, Porgy and his band try to hold the plantation by chasing off the minions of the law. Providentially, however, some powerful friends arrive and are able to prove that M'Kewn had cheated Porgy and hence has no legal claim. M'Kewn, exposed, commits suicide; and Porgy retires to a hopeful future on his gradually improving acres.

Porgy's plantation home stands at the center of this plot, and clearly Simms intends it to be a microcosm of the Southern agrarian system. Porgy himself, then, is an authentic example of the slaveholder—and one to be measured against Mrs. Stowe's Shelby, St. Clair, and Legree. Simms and other critics could retort to the undoubted emotional effectiveness of the brutal Legree by claiming that he was a notorious exception or by lamely pointing to the fact that Mrs. Stowe herself had made him a Yankee by birth. But Shelby and St. Clair are something else again; they are cast as Southerners, and Mrs. Stowe saw them as representative of their class. Kindly though they are, they are improvident; and their easygoing natures rather than their bad characters permit Uncle Tom to slip into the clutches of Legree.

In her portrayal, Mrs. Stowe had touched upon a sore point; as Simms well realized, the view of the Southern planter as a shiftless pleasure-seeker who drew his substance from the wasteful enslavement of downtrodden Negroes was widely held in the North. He had himself, moreover, portrayed Porgy in earlier volumes in much this way; the fat officer, though brave in military action, had often been revealed as a happy-go-lucky high liver. In *Woodcraft* Simms met this problem head on. Some unfavorable aspects of the South could be granted; but, so the story implies, they existed in the long-ago. The time of the action is, after all, 1782; Mrs. Stowe's hedonistic planters of 1852 were anachronisms.

This was Simms's motivation in developing his portrait of Porgy, for he gives him several long speeches which show that his own private history recapitulates some phases of the older South. In one revealing passage, for example, Simms allows Millhouse to upbraid Porgy for having wasted his inheritance in pleasant living. Porgy's frank reply does not spare himself:

"Pray believe that I was a very foolish, profligate person, who, in ceasing to be young, did not cease to be foolish, and continued his absurd vanities and excesses to the last. And I am telling you now, Millhouse, what has been but too commonly the case among our young men of fortune of my day. There were some exceptions, it is true; but the curse of my generation was that our fathers lived too well, were too rapidly prosperous, and though they did not neglect the exercise of a proper industry in themselves, they either did not know how to teach it to their children, or presumed on the absence of any necessity that they should learn. We were to be affluent in what they should leave us—enough, in God's name, if we could keep it—but it is very sure that the best way to teach one to value and to keep what he gets, is just to teach him how to get it himself. He who has not learned the one lesson will fail in the other, and is apt to waste what he did not work for . . ." (206).

This had been the fact, but the lesson has since been learned. The requirement, Porgy now knows, is a continuing responsibility, a refusal to accept as one's own anything which one has had no share in gaining or preserving. Porgy has had to discover the truth harshly: first, by recognizing that to keep the plantation way of life he must for a while give it up—go to war to protect the right of having had it at all. Secondly, he must return and rebuild it out of chaos, making it at last a true part of himself.

This theme of Porgy's rise to self-knowledge and responsibility is further underscored by his relationship with Millhouse and the Widow Eveleigh in the wooing plot. Porgy, like other Simms protagonists, reflects the cultured, aristocratic background of an older South, though he is a much more jovial type; Millhouse is a solid man of the middle class, gruff and practical in his manner. As has been seen, Simms had already dealt several times with this clash of personalities and the resultant benefits to both men. Millhouse is not entirely like the scouts of the earlier tales, but his thematic function is much the same: he counterbalances Porgy's sensual pleasure of gluttony and his pseudo-courtly fashion of speech.

Widow Eveleigh already combines the virtues of both types; she has the toughmindedness of the back country and the refinements of an old established family. Secure in her good breeding and in her estate, she can exhibit that quality which grows naturally out of her position: liberality. Yet she also demands responsibility in those who receive her bounty. And so she must reject Porgy's proposal of marriage because she knows that immediate convenience and not love has promoted it. In character and in practicality she is the strongest person in the book, and she would scorn (as Simms intends the reader to) the pallid wives of Mrs. Stowe's slaveowners: the kindly but ineffectual Mrs. Shelby and the incredibly self-centered Mrs. St. Clair.

Devotion to the Southern system is again set forth in Simms's treatment of the group who, as might be anticipated, play a vastly enlarged role in *Woodcraft*—the slaves. Here the "answer" to Mrs. Stowe is more explicit, since Simms brings Negro characters into nearly every chapter of the book except those which deal with the M'Kewn-Bostwick subplot. No slave, we observe, is ever ill-treated, none unhappy or uncared for, none unwilling to share the present hard lot of the leader class. Nor are slave families torn apart in the way which Mrs. Stowe had made so touchingly effective. Instead, expressions of mutual affection between master and slave abound, and several long episodes—including the return of a group who have been hiding

out in the swamps—accent the joys of reunion rather than the
sorrows of separation.

But the slave issue is most directly confronted in the numerous
dialogues between Porgy and his cook Tom. Their close relationship during wartime had been sketched in earlier volumes; here
it is developed as Tom returns to his normal station in plantation
life. Personal respect, outspokenness, the concern of each for the
other's physical welfare—these are the attributes which Simms
invites us to examine in a slave-based society; and he presses
his case by the dramatic method, rather than by authorial
comment. Could Porgy, out of his present necessity, bear to part
with Tom? His aide Lance brings up the question when he notes
that Porgy, as a debtor, is likely to have his slaves confiscated
for payment. Porgy's answer is meant to be a winning one:

> "I love Tom. Tom is virtually a free man. It's true, being a debtor,
> I can not confer freedom upon him. . . . [But if there is a
> danger of losing him]—then, I shall kill Tom, Lance; I'll shoot
> *him*—him, Tom—in order to save him. The poor fellow has
> faithfully served a gentleman. He shall never fall into the hands
> of a scamp. . . . Tom, I'm thinking, would rather die my slave,
> than live a thousand years under another owner" (113).

Was Simms calling to mind another slave named Tom, who
was sold unwillingly by a kind master only to come under the
power of a vicious one—and one who was not by birth a
Southerner? Whether intended as direct allusion to *Uncle Tom's
Cabin* or not, the contrast in owners' attitudes might well have
been remarked by a contemporary reader of both books. And
such a reader could scarcely have missed the scene in which
Tom orders a younger slave to lay a tablecloth for dinner. The
latter, looking around a room bare of furniture, complains: "I no
see any table, uncle Tom!" And Tom indignantly fires back:
"Don't you uncle me, you chucklehead!" (179).

Cleverly, Simms lets Tom have his own say at the very end
of the book, where his words might linger in a reader's memory.
Having settled his affairs, Porgy now offers Tom his freedom,
that goal so avidly sought by Eliza's husband George, and even
promised to Uncle Tom himself. The comment of Porgy's slave
is a neat condensation of several of *Woodcraft's* leading motifs:

"No! no! maussa," he cried, with a sly shake of the head, "I kain't t'ink ob letting you off dis way. Ef *I* doesn't b'long to *you, you* b'longs to *me!* You hab for keep dis nigger long as he lib; and him for keep you. You hab for fin' he dinner, and Tom hab for cook 'em. Free nigger no hab any body for fin' 'em he bittle [victuals]; and de man wha' hab sense and good maussa, at de same time, he's a d--n pretickilar great big fool, for let he maussa off from keep 'em and fin' 'em. I no guine to be free no way you kin fix it; so, maussa, don't you bodder me wid dis nonsense t'ing 'bout free paper any more. I's well off whar' I is I tell you; and I much rudder [rather] b'long to good maussa, wha' I lub, dan be my own maussa and quarrel wid mese'f ebbry day. Da's it! You yerry now? I say de wud for all! *You* b'longs to *me*, Tom, jes' as much as me Tom b'long to *you;* and you nebber guine git *you* free paper from me long as you lib" (509). [The brackets and italics are Simms's.]

Mrs. Stowe's Uncle Tom goes to glory with the marks of Legree's fatal beating upon him; but Simms's Tom, lucky to have a true *Southern* master, remains until his death Porgy's "cook and proprietor."

In *Woodcraft* Simms made his reply to Mrs. Stowe both explicit and implicit. Most explicit, of course, was the presentation of Porgy as solicitous master. This portrayal was clear-cut, and many Southern readers would have echoed Hammond's judgment that Simms had "admirably defended our 'Institution.'" If this were all that the romance accomplished, it could easily be relegated to a place among the countless tracts of Southern apologists. And yet in this book Simms also managed to present a view of the South as a responsible society, one misunderstood and misrepresented by the North. No mere defensive tract-writer, he endeavored to give a positive dramatic rendering of a region which, he argued, had been the victim of ignorant abolitionists. In carrying out this aim, he produced what is his most coherent and cogent single work of fiction. However much we may now despise the views that he expressed, it would be hard to argue that he boasted unreasonably when he said that his story was "as good an answer to Mrs. Stowe" as the South was capable of producing.[4]

CHAPTER 8

The South Triumphant

I *Southward Ho!*

SIMMS'S reawakened interest in the Revolution prompted him to carry on the story in two more romances: *The Forayers* (1855) and *Eutaw* (1856). But before they reached print another period of extreme labor and personal hardship was to pass. He finally threw off the irritating burden of editing the *Southern Quarterly Review* at the end of 1854; but even with this pressure removed his remaining tasks were enough to exhaust any average writer. Most urgent among these was the preparation of what has remained to this day the standard edition of his works—the collection of tales and poems begun in 1853 under the imprint of J. S. Redfield of New York. A comparison of the Redfield edition of *The Yemassee* with its original version, for example, reveals that Simms's changes for this "new and revised" series were generally not extensive; he rephrased here and there and corrected obvious errors, but the overall form remained much the same. Much more comprehensive were his additions to his original prefaces; these offer many useful insights into Simms's evaluations of his earlier efforts from the viewpoint of a long-established author.

In addition to toiling over these revisions, Simms published two other works of fiction before *The Forayers* and *Eutaw*. The first of these, *Vasconselos* (1853), is concerned with the wanderings of De Soto and with the death of the explorer on the banks of the Mississippi. Hoping to see whether it was his name or stories themselves that sold copies, Simms issued *Vaconselos* under the pseudonym "Frank Cooper"; when it gained a medium success, he admitted his authorship. But this tale is no more convincing than his previous tired reworkings of foreign material; we pass by it with merely a nod.

The second of these books, *Southward Ho!*, is more entertaining, but it must also be adjudged a minor pot-boiler. In form it is, as Simms described it, a "sort of Decameron—a thread of circumstance, upon which I hung my scattered fabrications" (*L*, III, 355). The setting is a steamer voyaging from New York to Charleston; the individual stories, all written some time before, are told by the passengers to relieve the tedium of the trip. Simms made a slight effort to fit a story to the timetable of the journey; the sight of the New Jersey coast, for example, brings out an account of a notorious "wrecker." But the total effect of the book is a hodgepodge. By far the most noteworthy sections are those dealing with the voyage itself, since in them Simms flaunted a more brazen Southern nationalism than he had permitted himself in other works of fiction. The recent secessionist sentiment in South Carolina was much on his mind in these narrative divisions; in several passages he sets up a representative of his own state to argue the political situation with other Southerners and to directly bait the North. One of these occasions is a Fourth of July celebration; after several windy orations, including one by a tipsy Alabamian who savages New England for its stand against slavery, the party proceeds to the offering of toasts. Two of these, particularly, betray Simms's now fiery mood:

> *The Slave States of the South.*—The conservators of the peace, where faction never rears its head, where mobs tear not down, nor burn, nor destroy the hopes and habitations of the peaceful and weak, and where reverence in the people is still the guarantee for a gentleman in the politician.

> *Our Slaves.*—Like our children, minors in the hands of the guardian, to be protected and trained to usefulness and virtue— to be taught service and obedience—love and loyalty—to be nurtured with a care that never wrongs, and governed by a rule that simply restrains the excesses of humanity.[1]

Dozens of sentiments like these could be culled from the pages of *Southward Ho!*, but the effort would be pointless since they merely echo the familiar shrill cries of Southern patriots. What is of value in the book is its specific demonstration that, when Simms directly raised the practical issue of Southern nationalism in a contemporary setting, his tone became strident and pugnacious. Some of this bellicosity he was to carry over into *The Forayers* and *Eutaw*. But in these two romances he was moving not in a world of immediate political upheavals but in one of the imagination. The whole idea of the South was raised from the level of plotting to that of historical speculation. In so elevating his treatment, Simms moved from the straight pamphleteering of *Southward Ho!* to what is nearer to being literary art.

II *The Battle of Eutaw*

The Forayers, or, The Raid of the Dog-Days and its sequel, *Eutaw*, were conceived by Simms as a unit and may conveniently be discussed together. Running to 1,142 pages, the two books represent Simms's most sustained effort in fiction; and, in closing out his multivolumed narrative of the Revolution, they stand as a capstone to his career. That Simms himself considered them as a grand finale is borne out by two facts. First, in the preface to *The Forayers*, he reviews the actual course of the Revolution, relates his books to that history, and congratulates himself that he has been able to achieve his purpose of illustrating the "social condition of the country" during those times.[2] Second, he brings briefly onto the stage a number of the leading characters of the earlier volumes—among them, Singleton, Mellichampe, and Porgy; the effect is to emphasize the "epic" aspect of the entire series. It is true that one more long work—*The Cassique of Kiawah* (1859)—remained to be published and that his letters show that Simms at least contemplated adding other scenes to his Southern cycle.[3] All that he completed after *Eutaw*, however, falls far below the standard achieved in the seven-volume saga.

Though *Woodcraft*, the immediately preceding tale, was concerned with the postwar period, Simms saw that the final two sections better rounded off the chief themes of the series—the war which the colonials fought both against the British and themselves and the gradual growth of the Southern system. Almost all the minor motifs and many of the plot devices also make a reappearance. On a first reading, then, one may gain the impression that Simms was merely dishing up a salable stock-in-trade; more careful examination shows that he was not just recapitulating but was actually offering a reconsidered view of his society.

The Forayers and *Eutaw* deal in their historical aspects with the "raid of the dog-days"—partisan attacks on the British regulars—and with the culminating and decisive battle of Eutaw Springs. The military action of these scorching summer months of 1781 provides the general backdrop, but far less often than in earlier tales does Simms take the field with his guerilla bands. British power is now everywhere on the wane; raiders have captured many of the posts long held by the enemy; and Southerners who have remained loyal to the crown are having chilling second thoughts. As final victory looms, Simms turns the reader's attention not so much to the British enemy as to the personalities of the natives who have been engaged in the struggle on both sides.

The plots of these two long books are developed in a leisurely fashion and are extended by many minor complications; but there is no point in a detailed summary, for one theme is paramount throughout: Simms's demonstration that the real difference between the loyalist and the revolutionary Southerner lies in the individual's attitude toward life, in his concept of what social structure in the South ought ideally to be. Simms divides most of his characters into positive and negative thinkers. The latter type clings to a traditional and sometimes corrupted view of community; the former is the new and developing order which will take the best from the past (thus preserving continuity) but which will scorn many of the precepts of the passing generation and will strenuously resist those hangers-on who value only materialistic standards.

Simms most clearly dramatizes this clash in several meetings between the partisan Major Willie Sinclair and his loyalist father. Colonel Sinclair is an Englishman of a former day, a hero who served gallantly in wars with the Indians; now, however, he is compelled by age and the gout to sit about on his ancestral plantation and curse the American upstarts who have had the gall to engage the king's regulars. As will be recalled, the situation is similar to the dissention between Singleton and Colonel Walton in *The Partisan;* what is new is the closer blood tie and the fact that Colonel Sinclair undergoes a more explicit character change than did Colonel Walton. Colonel Sinclair may

strike some readers as one more stock figure—that sort of noble
old gentleman whom adherents of the Lost Cause were later to
view through a steam of sentimentality. Simms's own comment
on Sinclair, though, is a pointed corrective:

> Col. Sinclair was one of the despots of the old school; a gentle-
> man no doubt among gentlemen; but a lord to all others;—a man
> capable of generosity in high degree, and condescension; but
> one who expected that you should understand his condescension,
> and feel his generosity. He was, really, a person of a century
> even older than his own; and though he fully believed in Adam
> and Eve, as the parents of that prolific family vulgarly recognised
> as the human, yet no priesthood in the world could have per-
> suaded him that there were not a great many varieties of clay
> employed in the moulding of those myriad varieties which
> constitute the sum total of the races of men! He had swayed as
> a superior so long, and as a natural superior, that it was not
> possible with him to question his own legitimacy, or to acknowl-
> edge the claims of that fungus multitude, which it needed
> another hundred years to raise, in any degree, to a fairly human
> position . . . (*F*, 109).

Simms usually refers to the colonel as "the baron" and to
his estate as "the barony," terms which hark back to the colonial
land grants and to John Locke's scheme for a native aristocracy.
His "nobility," thus, is ancient and transmissible, but he has
neglected a concomitant inheritance: *noblesse oblige.* He cannot
appreciate that for all his wealth, his family background, his
training, and his experience, he must himself keep earning the
right to remain a leader. But his son Willie, like others in the
rising generation, accepts continued responsibility as the central
principle of an ordered society; though he respects his father
and always treats him with proper deference, he finds that he
must oppose the old man on many doctrines which the colonel
thinks forever unchangeable. It is true that Willie is a revolutionary, that he has raised arms against his king; but at least his
father, a seasoned warrior, can give grudging praise to his
bravery in the field. The son, however, has dared to act even
further against the father's code: he would marry the daughter
of a lower-class supplier to the British troops. Though the colonel
finds the politics of this supplier, Captain Travis, thoroughly
sound, the man is unquestionably common. Self-made and

now well off, Travis himself had wed into a class a step above his own; outwardly, he has been living an entirely respectable life. But his daughter, Bertha, must necessarily (in the colonel's view) carry the low blood of her father; to have it intermingled with that of the Sinclairs is unthinkable.

Willie is determined to stand up to his father on this crucial point, and in his plea for Bertha he makes the most stirring appeal for "natural nobility" that Simms ever wrote. The scene in which he recites his credo requires quotation at length. Having admitted to his sister Carrie that the rumors of his love are true, Willie now faces her reproaches. The aghast Carrie asks, Could he really want to link himself with a family beneath his own? Willie warmly responds that the Travises are not low in anything that should count and that he will not sacrifice his happiness to pure class prejudice. Bewildered, Carrie inquires, "But you surely, Willie, acknowledge the claim of caste and society?" Willie's rejoinder is delivered in bravura rhetoric, but Simms's own underlying sincerity helps redeem its phrasing:

> "To be sure I do, Carrie; but not when they err, and do wrong to claims which are not less legitimate than their own! I'll tell you where they err, Carrie; in their inflexible resolve never to recognise those exceptional cases which are rightly acknowledged always, as such, even when we obey the rule. Caste and class properly pride themselves upon the habitual refinements of mind and moral, acquired in long periods of time. This constitutes their just claim to authority; and they rightly hold themselves aloof from associations with other classes, who do not know, and do not properly value these refinements. But there is, here and there, a natural nobility in individuals, which overrides the law, and demands recognition. There are persons to whom refinement is *native*—who are *born* nobles—delicate and just in sentiment, magnanimous in soul, generous in courage, endowed with noble talents, and devoted to noble purposes. It is the duty of an aristocracy to acknowledge all such persons, as soon as found, and take them lovingly into their embrace, and seek to do them honor; and there is a twofold wisdom in doing so, since we thus add to our own resources of society, and increase our influence upon mankind at large. But classes are apt to show themselves too jealous of position, and too slow to recognise these occasional claims of the individual. The consequence is that they make him hostile; and he will bring his natural powers to bear

against them—will expose their weaknesses, and revenge upon
them his own hurts of self-esteem—an injustice that always
avenges itself upon the wrong-doer; and, in the end, we pay
a double penalty; forced not only, at last, to acknowledge the
claims to which we unwisely opposed ourselves at first, but
to pay them tribute also, and to submit to an authority which
becomes exacting and despotic in proportion to the tenacity
with which it has been resisted and denied. No one, more highly
than myself, esteems the claims of social caste. It is a natural
condition, and rightly possesses authority; but, God forbid! that
I should sullenly and sternly reject the occasional individual,
whose personal claims put him above his condition in society!
He has received from nature his badges of nobility, and society
is simply ridiculous when it opposes itself to the credentials
which come patent from the hands of God himself! Be assured
that, in all such conflicts, the class refusing to acknowledge the
individual only proves itself unworthy, and perils all the securities
upon which it prides itself" (*F*, 86-87).

This concept of a natural aristocracy—of a social framework
flexible enough to allow the individual of fundamental worth
to rise, no matter what his origins—is not novel in Simms's
fiction; it had been implicit in his treatment of such scouts as
Jack Bannister and Thumbscrew Witherspoon. What is distinctive here is that the principle is developed in numerous explicit
bits of action; throughout all the gradations of society Simms
shows change in operation—the new order in the actual process
of becoming.

First, on the highest level of rank, Simms renders this evolutionary development by contrasting Colonel Sinclair with his
earlier counterpart, Colonel Walton. The latter, the reader will
remember, had taken the British protection but had achieved
redemption through death, through the sacrifice of self. For
Colonel Sinclair, salvation comes through his finally accepting
a new life, through acknowledging that he must pay allegiance
to a new flag. Pressing his theme, Simms arranges for the
Colonel's transformation by means of the very person who had
come between him and his son—Bertha Travis.

As actual fighting nears their homes, old Sinclair, Carrie, and
also the Travises (mother and daughter) take flight. After many
escapades the Travises find refuge in a remote cottage. The

Colonel and Carrie have similar narrow escapes, but by chance are rescued by the Travises and brought to the same hideout. It is here that the Colonel's shift of character begins. First, he is shaken by his new knowledge of British defeats: Can he have been wrong about the supposed invincibility of the king's troops? Has the mother country been unjust in her attempt to subjugate the colonials? Second, what is he to think of this mother and daughter who have saved him? The Travis women, recognizing the Colonel (who has never seen them before), have decided to remain incognito and have adopted the name "Smith," since they know of his prejudice toward Bertha. But even with their name against them the Colonel has been attracted, observing their bearing, proper manners, and Bertha's beauty and intelligence. How could such qualities of the high born exist in such low people?

It takes a heroic effort of will for the Colonel to arrive at the proper answers, but he begins the venture in a tortured conversation with his daughter. Recalling that during their flight he had (without knowing who his intended victim was) fired at his son, the Colonel reflects dolefully:

"I have been harsh to Willie! How harsh, I only begun to feel when I had lifted weapon against his life. What a madness was that! And why should I have been harsh to him? . . . True, he had joined the rebel cause! But the world changes. Laws change. Nations change. There must be change among men and nations, for they are mortal. There have been revolutions enough in Britain, and who was right? The present house was not that which ruled my fathers. Was I not a rebel, too, when I gave my allegiance to the Guelph [member of a German princely family], the house of Stuart having still a living representative? Yet I feel justified. Why? What is the argument? Not worth a straw! And how should he care for either? This is a new world, and why should it not have its own dynasties? Why not a new race in authority *here*—as proper as any in Britain? . . . So be it! Let Willie choose his own master. I forgive him the rebellion. He is faithless to no duty, which, as a son, he owes to me! And what was his other offence? He would choose a wife to suit himself, not me! Ah! Carrie, what had I to do with that? Could I doubt that, good, brave, noble fellow, as he is, with cultivated mind, and generous heart, and nice sensibilities, he would choose wisely and well? It was that devil of pride which I have too much nurtured, which roused me up, in that matter, to such fierce hostility. . . . Let the boy marry whom he pleases! I should not quarrel with him, *now,* were he even to declare for this gentle little creature, with the plebeian name of Smith . . ." (*E,* 414-15).

It does not take much imagination to guess what Simms's denouement now will be, but this is not a sudden fifth-act conversion of a cruel papa in sentimental drama. Indeed, the speech—with its recognition of a son's right to rebel and to "choose his own master"—has thoroughly subversive overtones. So far Simms's daring could go in this year of 1856: "There must be change among men and nations."

Colonel Sinclair's conversion from loyalty to secession is paralleled in the career of Captain Travis. The Captain is that familiar type in the Revolutionary romances, the native American of the lower middle class who supports the British because of greed for spoils and not because of principle. A good share of Travis' profit has not been legitimate even by the enemy's standards. He has been falsifying his accounts to get money for objects that are more exalted than he ought to aspire to: a fine house and slaves to wait upon his higher-born wife and their children. His peculations have been discovered by Captain Inglehardt, another American who has risen to a commission in the British service despite his humble birth. Inglehardt, like Travis, has straightforward pecuniary lusts; and, like Travis too, he wants to improve his social status by a good marriage—with Travis' daughter Bertha. His hope lies in blackmail; he will not report Travis to the British if the latter will consent to the wedding.

This demand is too much even for Travis; he pretends to accede but calls in Willie Sinclair and asks for a formal transfer to the American side. The wily Inglehardt, however, learns of this double-dealing and makes Travis and his young son prisoners in a backwoods hideout; they will be released only if Travis orders an immediate marriage. Continued captivity and a resolute attempt not to submit drive Travis insane; and, in his crazed attack upon Inglehardt, both he and his captor receive fatal wounds.

Behind this melodramatic bit of business Simms's thematic line is again plain. Though Travis has repented and turned to the patriots, as has Colonel Sinclair, his original motivation for espousing the British side was self-seeking and not, as with Sinclair, a matter of training and inherited belief. Travis must die to purge himself of his past; nothing he can now do will help to save him except the negative virtue of not committing further wickednesses. Inglehardt, however, is beyond any sort of redemption; he is cold, aloof, unfeeling except for what he frankly calls his "passions" for Bertha. Never getting so far as to admit his evil-doing, he must meet death in all his depravity. Both men have tried to turn the Revolutionary movement into a game run for personal profit; as their deaths make certain, they have cheated finally only themselves.

Travis and Inglehardt at least were intelligent and craftily ambitious. But even this much cannot be said for the outlaw bands whose villainous activities are chronicled throughout these two tales. These marauders are not only vicious and greedy; they are mentally incapable of comprehending that any moral order exists except their own gang spirit. On the whole they are accounted loyalists, but they serve only when the king's troops are in the ascendency. Taking advantage of the disruption of wartime, they prey upon rebel, Tory, and Briton alike whenever they get the chance.

This problem of the person who sets himself outside established law, who accepts no responsibility for his behavior, long obsessed Simms. In story after story he returned to the type and exposed as many of its facets as convention allowed him to. Partly, Simms depicted such dark rogues to gratify the tastes of his readers; but on a more serious thematic level they were intended to symbolize the result of a social order in disruption. They were to be expected in the South Carolina of the Revolutionary period; they were equally to be watched for in the raw Alabama settlements of *Richard Hurdis*. But they could not survive indefinitely; when the community structure became solidified, such terrorists would have to depart.

What would insure the downfall of the marauder, these two romances suggest, was to be the extension of education in its broadest sense—the inculcation in all ranks of a belief in the necessity for finding one's rightful place. Learning had to be made available to all—not only so that the "natural noble" might rise but also so that those of inferior capabilities might be made conscious of their duties. For too long a time, Simms intimates, education had been the prerogative of the wealthy; in an ideal South every man must at least have the chance to develop his mind as far as possible.

Simms presents this point in a curious way in a scene in *Eutaw* by putting his sentiments into the mouth of one of the blackest scoundrels in his gallery, an outlaw leader called Hell-Fire Dick. Dick has been ordered by Inglehardt to stand guard over Travis' young son Henry and to starve him slowly so that the father will give in and permit the marriage with Bertha. But Dick has begun to display an unexpected weakness; he has grown to like Henry—who has inherited the high qualities of his mother—and he is unnerved by the way his cruel treatment is weakening the boy. In a remarkable passage, Dick reveals his uneasiness to other members of the gang:

"I'd rather we could fix it so as to make the starvation fall on the father, rather than that young cock; for I like the fellow. He's got a big heart in his leetle buzzom, and it rather goes agin me to harness him down so tight. But we've got to squeeze somebody to get the gould. We kain't do without that. Even the buzzards must be fed, you know."

"But a man ought to git better feeding than a buzzard, Dick."

"En so I'm thinking all the time; but how's it that one man will get the feed of twenty, and another won't git his own poor share of one, though he has all the trouble and the resk? It's owing to the harrystocracy that keeps all the book-l'arning to themselves. That's the how. I wonder, when the fighting's done, how we're to git along? . . . What's to become of we all? That's the puzzle. As for me, I do believe I'm not good for nothing but skrimmaging."

"And I don't see, old fellow," quoth Brunson, "that skrimmaging ever did much *for you*, more than scouting for me! It filled your pockets one day, may be; but somebody else came along the next, and skrimmaged you empty again."

"Ah! it's owing to the want of book-l'arning. Them harrys-tocrats keep all the books to themselves; but we'll see! I reckon books ain't hard to l'arn, after all; for, you sees, a poor leetle brat of a boy, knee-high to a young turkey—why, he kin l'arn to read, and spell, and write; and I don't see what's to hender a grown man from book-l'arning, when he knows so much more than a boy. It ought to be more easy to him" (*E*, 247-48).

Dick's new realization of one of the distinctions of class takes a surprising turn. Having seized a book from an old woman so that he can get Henry to teach him to read, he becomes absorbed in the story of that book—*Pilgrim's Progress.* The scene could now be developed sentimentally; Dick could be won over by the allegory and, repentent, help the Travises to get away. But Simms manages his climax with an ironic twist. *Pilgrim's Progress* literally saves Dick; the volume, which he carries in a breast pocket, stops a bullet during a battle. But while Dick is marvelling over this odd escape he relaxes his vigilance; and Willie Sinclair, on his way to rescue the Travises, slays him. He is killed off, one gathers, because he is so base and stupid that his preservation for the postwar world is impossible. He is right that "book-l'arning" is indispensable, but the education of which he speaks so wistfully simply represents for him one of the factors which make men "harrystocrats." He cannot see that more knowledge for him would mean acceptance of his place in the lower ranks.

Several other minor characters in *The Forayers* and in *Eutaw* merit some comment. First is the scout, who makes his final appearance in the person of one of Sinclair's aides, Jim Ballou. Jim is as adept at woodcraft as any of his prototypes, and he has the old frontier pride in his abilities:

> "I know my business—foxing, snaking, moling, cooning, possum-ing, and, if need be, wolfing!—these being the six degrees, in all of which, to be worth anything, a scout's got to graduate! But he's to be born to it, besides. These are natural gifts. Education can improve 'em, no doubt, but can't create them! Remember that, brother, remember that—remember!" (*E,* 114)

Jim, however, has a taint that afflicted none of the other woodsmen: he is addicted to the bottle, especially to "Jimmaker" rum. Nor is this a mere off-duty thirst; he has recently been caressing the jug while tracking, and his folly has allowed him to be trailed by the enemy into one of the partisans' secret hide-outs. Willie Sinclair's impulse is to relieve him at once from duty, but Jim swears his "celestial" oath never to touch another drop. For the remainder of the story he sticks to this resolve, though not without the tortures of withdrawal, and he wins back Willie's confidence. He is not basically bad but humanly weak, and he can rehabilitate himself as Hell-Fire Dick cannot. It is interesting to note here the reversal in the usual roles of the young nobleman and the scout. As the war moves to its close in these two books, Simms does not allow Willie to act foolishly; on the other hand, he does tone down the occasionally priggish manner of the frontiersman. Relieved of the necessity of playing mentor to the hero, the scout can be permitted a vice which would have been out of the question in his predecessors.

Significant also among the minor characters are the slaves. Simms describes several of them at length in his opening pages, and shows one as bravely fighting alongside the partisans. Later in the story he gives a conspicuous role to Cato, the body-servant and guard of the two Travis women. Cato is either seen in animated action, fighting to keep them from capture, or, in quieter moments, exerting his influence in lordly fashion over the other Negroes. As *Woodcraft* revealed, Simms had found it expedient to defend the slave system somewhat obliquely. But he did, in *The Forayers,* allow himself one aside that is typical of his attitude in the year 1855. Cato was, Simms informs us,

> the only *family* negro whom Travis, as a *novus homo* could claim. He had inherited Cato in right of his wife, and, as an old family negro, the fellow was held to be faithful. This was the usual characteristic of the class. It was the *"new* negro"—the African fresh from the coast, whom it was found good policy always to distrust. Cato was not simply faithful. He was sternly and bravely so. He was fearless in the assertion of the rights of his "young missis," by which title he continued to recognise the mother of Bertha, long after the latter had entered her teens. To both, and to his master, Cato never hesitated to offer his opinions, and if necessary, his rebuke. As if conscious of his integrity and of its recognition in the family, he asserted his moral rights under it, and was just as frequently guardian and censor, in his province, as body-servant or carriage-driver [*F*, 480].

So much for Mrs. Stowe! Would the passage have been noticed by a contemporary reader? It seems likely, especially when one considers the fact that Simms is turning the point of *Uncle Tom's Cabin* upside-down. Not only is there no mention of possible physical chastisement of the noble Cato; it is *he* who "if necessary" offers his "rebuke." He is a part, and an integral one, of Simms's society—he knows his place, accepts his duties, and takes in turn his own rights from his superiors. For Cato there is no possible change of status, no movement toward freedom; he is already as solidly right in the South's scheme as is Willie Sinclair.

A full analysis of *The Forayers* and *Eutaw* would require at least a look at some of the other figures in Simms's extended cast. There is, for example, the clairvoyant Harricane Nell, the outwardly wild but entirely innocent girl who races through the action on her swamp pony, spreading her warnings of disaster.[4] There are also new studies of the poor-white class in Pete Blodgit and his harridan mother. But a discussion of these two romances must limit itself at some point, and enough has been said to indicate what Simms intended in the final installments of the Revolutionary series. To quote what he remarked at the beginning of *The Forayers*, it had been his plan to give an overall view of the South during the campaigns of the War of Independence; but he also wished to make those military actions subordinate "to other events, [and] . . . to illustrate the social condition of the country, under the influence of those strifes and trials which give vivacity to ordinary circumstances, and mark with deeper hues, and stronger colors, and sterner tones, the otherwise common progress of human hopes and fears, passions and necessities" [F, 5].

The grand movement from *The Partisan* through *Eutaw* had been from despair to hope, from military defeat to a South triumphant in arms. Simms had portrayed all levels of society and he had interconnected them by one central theme: the responsibility of each to all in the establishment of a lasting system. The "epic" period was over; now it was time for physical rebuilding, for the growth of the nation within a nation. It was time, in other words, for Simms's contemporary South to make its appearance on the stage of world history as a potentially ideal social order.

CHAPTER 9

"I Am a Southron"

I   A Cold North Wind

T HE NOTICES of *The Forayers* and *Eutaw* were on the whole approving, and Simms received the gratifying news that they were enjoying good sales. Moreover, the Redfield collected set was well under way; and he was once more back in the spotlight in the role he most relished—that of the popular chronicler of his state.[1] But in spite of this renewed recognition of his talents for historical fiction, Simms now sensed that the major phase of his career was over; several of his letters convey this feeling of a task completed, though he was in 1856 only fifty years old and still mentally and physically vigorous. His own mood is echoed in a letter from his Carolina friend Hammond, sent shortly after the appearance of the final two Revolutionary romances. Hammond, always a shrewd critic of Simms, carped about points of plot and characterization, but he was not at all stinting in his praise of their general effect. Yet even he concluded his comments with this suggestion: "If I were you I would now cease to write novels. You can't better these last & may never again do so well. Your fame might safely repose on these if all the others were destroyed" (*L*, III, 425, n. 36).

These premonitions were borne out by Simms's subsequent career. Though he was to publish one more long romance, *The Cassique of Kiawah*, in 1859, and though he returned to the subject of the Revolution in serial stories written in the late 1860's, he never again produced a long work of fiction comparable to *Woodcraft* or *The Forayers*. It is difficult to state positively the reasons behind this long decline, but a few of the factors are clear. First, as always, there was his acute financial problem. Publication costs were now much higher than they had been at the beginning of his career, and the return—even on a good sale—was so comparatively small as to make him doubt whether it was worth the research and sheer writing labor that had gone into his recent productions. Moreover, he was now but one of a throng of popular romancers; no longer could he make the claim that he was putting fresh materials before the public. But if the matter of poorer royalties had to be considered it was not in itself decisive. For other changes had come over America; the split between North and South was widening, and Simms was not so eager as he had been to appeal to a wide national audience. In 1853, when the first volumes in the Redfield edition came off the presses, Simms might have been surprised that anyone could find his celebration of the South truly offensive. But, after a disagreeable experience in the fall of 1856, his awareness of increasing Northern hostility to his views became acute.

The occasion for this painful awakening was a projected lecture tour of several Northern cities. For some years Simms had been supplementing his income by speaking throughout the South. His topics were generally literary, historical, and philosophical—disquisitions on "The Moral Character of Hamlet," "Ante-Colonial History of the South," or "Poetry and the Practical."[2] With such experience behind him, he saw no bar to similar success in the North; and so in April, 1856, he sounded out Evert A. Duyckinck and other Northern friends.[3] The response was immediate and warm; old acquaintances invited him not only to give public lectures but also to make more intimate talks before historical, literary, and cultural societies. In every way the tour promised to be both "desirable to others, & compensative" to himself (L, III, 429).

Simms began his scheduled circuit in Buffalo, New York, on the night of November 11, 1856. His subject was one well calculated to draw readers of his romances—"South Carolina in the Revolution"—and he was gratified as he stepped onto the platform to find that more than 1,200 auditors had crowded into the hall. Obviously he had originally intended to do a service for his native state by showing how much more it had contributed to the Revolutionary cause than Northern historians had granted. He would pay tribute to the partisan leaders, describe the battles that drove the British to defeat at Yorktown, detail the privations and heroism of the Carolinians in combating an enemy that had been the foe of the Northern colonies as well. All this, in a sense, he did accomplish. But his manner was an appalling miscalculation. In a forensic style that sounded as if he were prosecuting the ruffian assailants of a widowed mother, he turned every phrase in praise of South Carolina into a vicious thrust at New England. From opening sentence into heated peroration, his tone was variously contentious, gibing, insulting. The reaction of listeners who had come to hear a literary man speak on a favorite subject must have been close to complete bewilderment.

Their surprise might have been less if they had known Simms the man better, or if they had more fully appreciated certain events which had helped to stimulate this remarkable diatribe. For, just a few months earlier, a scene had taken place on the United States Senate floor which to Simms symbolized all the past clashes between the North and his place of birth. In a speech during the Kansas debate, Senator Charles Sumner of Massachusetts had made disparaging remarks about South Carolina and about its then senator, Andrew Pickens Butler. Two days later Butler's nephew, Representative Preston Smith Brooks, walked into the Senate chamber and severely beat Sumner with a cane; Sumner did not fully recover from his injuries for more than three years. The incident naturally stirred up resentment in both sections of the nation; that it also left bruises upon Simms was inevitable.

When, therefore, Simms appeared before his Buffalo audience, he approached his topic as a second avenger of Butler. For eighty years, he told his listeners, the people of South Carolina had been secure in "the faith that the fame of their ancestors was beyond reproach"—that no one could diminish the deeds of the Revolutionary patriots.[4] But now a senator had arisen in Washington—Simms did not name Sumner directly—and proclaimed that the South Carolinians had been "false to their duties & their country . . . traitors in the cabinet and cowards in the field!" (521). Could this slur be justified? Simms asked; then he turned at once to demolish the charge. The numerous facts which Simms adduced concerning South Carolina's role might possibly have impressed his listeners and might even have made them consider that Sumner's aspersions had been unfair. But Simms could not avoid the personal argument, and the constantly reiterated word "Massachusetts" became in his speech an equivalent for the vilest and most despicable object. Moreover, he now directly argued what his romances had only implied: that South Carolinians of the past and the present were one continuing people; an attack upon one was an assault upon the other. His state, he said, could not accept the Northern affront supinely. Rising to near-hysteria in his conclusion, Simms all but declared the Civil War already opened:

> If there is to be strife between our respective countries [the word is significant]—if the future is to witness a conflict among ourselves—and this great empire be doomed to the convulsions of Civil War,—let the issues be unmixed; simple, single, unconfounded! If South Carolina, imbecile in the Past—be *now* imbecile—no matter from what cause—there need be no effort to prove the fact by argument. It will prove itself, in action! . . . Let the Future declare itself in its grimmest aspect, I shall not fear for her [South Carolina's] deportment in the worst of seasons. As neither Massachusetts, nor any other State, will gain any thing of honour when they lend a too eager [hand] to the defamation of the Past of South Carolina, so, be sure, the profit will be quite as small from her contemplated destruction in the future. If her doom is written, be equally sure, that she will fall no easy victim. With her lithe and sinewy limbs & muscles, she will twine herself around the giant caryatides which sustain the anchor of the great Confederacy [*i.e.*, the United States], and falling like the strong man of Israel, will bring down with her, in a common ruin, the vast and wondrous fabric, which her own prowess has so much helped to raise. Then, if there shall be one surviving sister, sitting solitary in the desolation, she will remain a monument, more significant of ruin than all the wreck which grows around her—the trophy of a moral desolation, which, by perversity and wrong, by a base selfishness which knew not how to be just, or how to be human, has with fratricidal hand, destroyed all its own securities and hopes—a moral suicide.—Forgive me, my friends, if I have spoken warmly; but you would not, surely, have me speak coldly in the assertion of a Mother's honour! (548-49)

As the historian Charles S. Sydnor has remarked, "Surely, Southerners had come a long way from Jefferson and a long way out of reality."[5] For the reaction to his polemic was what anyone in the lecture hall save Simms himself could have predicted. Though his audience heard him out, the storm broke in newspaper reviews of the speech. The crowd had come to hear a writer and not a politician; they had wanted to be pleasantly instructed—and had been subjected to the diatribe of a Southern fire-eater.[6] With such an unfriendly reception as this, it took real hardihood for Simms to repeat these views in public, first in Rochester and then in New York City. But the hostility of New York proved too much; and on November 21, just ten days after he began the trip for which he had held such hopes, he wrote to his hosts that he was canceling the rest of his engagements. He had communicated with his committee on arrangements and had been informed that "such is the antipathy felt to my topics,—such the rancourous feeling which they have provoked,—that they (the committee) could not only sell no tickets, but could not succeed in *giving* them away" (*L*, III, 458-59).

Amazed and heartsore, Simms returned to his plantation to brood; and on December 8 he tried to vindicate his actions to Hammond. This letter is striking for its revelation that Simms was not only unrepentant but totally uncomprehending. There was nothing in his lecture, so he told Hammond,

> which should have given offence. I forbore wherever I could to say what was offensive. . . . I made no allusion to Brooks, directly or indirectly. I did to Sumner, as the wanton assailant of S.C. . . . I had to do this, in order to show why, & on what points, I had undertaken to correct the vulgar mistakes or mis-representations of her history. But such is the rancorous temper of Black republicanism; so completely does New England rule N.Y.; and so malignantly do they all regard S.C., that the very subject re-aroused all the hostility. . . . My *heart* (suffer me to have one) was *slavishly* in these topics of S.C. I could no more fling them off from it, than I could fly. And my mind followed my heart. In this field, I was the champion; and my heroism did not stop to ask whether I should ever win thanks or a smile from the disdainful sovereign whom I was prepared to serve with my life . . . [*L*, III, 465-66; 469].

"My mind followed my heart" is the key to this sorry affair. As the reader has seen, Simms's identification of South Carolina's Revolutionary cause with its own present desire to go its in-dependent way had led to a curious emotional state; his own vision of a perfectible Southern order had blinded him to some immediate practicalities. He had, in his romances, created a South which in its ideal virtues was worthy to lead the whole nation to a new destiny. If the North refused to follow this shining guide, then the South had to take the course alone.

But did Simms actually believe that the South would be permitted to break off its connection with the Union by simply defying and renouncing the claims of the Northern states? Apparently he did. "If we are firm," he wrote to Hammond some time later, "yet not exacting, they will recede" (*L*, IV, 19). And he implored another friend, "Let all your game lie in the constant recognition & assertion of a *Southern Nationality!*" (*L*, III, 518). Armed conflict he naturally saw as a possible result of this intransigence. But was war inevitable? Until about 1860, so his letters prove, he kept to the view that the South could move as it pleased and that there would be no open battles unless the North foolheartedly invaded and attempted to subjugate the South—as the British had tried and failed to do earlier. Moreover, the whole plan of the lecture tour suggests that Simms hoped that the North could be educated to a degree to accept Southern institutions; he felt that, by some such effort as he was making, at least a few of the more intelligent Northerners would appreciate the Southern way of reasoning. But "my mind followed my heart." He was not being reasonable; he was an orator, attempting to move, to exhort, to proselytize. In truth, Simms had fallen victim to his own myth-making powers. To him the Southern nation was now, as it had been in the War of Independence, invincible and indestructible. If the North would not be taught, why let it beware! For if it attacked, it faced inevitable defeat. If it allowed the South to take its contemplated step of secession, then both nations could live in peace if not precisely in harmony. It was a strange sort of blindness, but the light was soon to come. It would begin in the flashes of gunfire around a fort which bore a name he had so often celebrated in his Revolutionary romances—Sumter.

II   *The End of a Dream*

The career of Simms from the mid-1850's to his death in 1870 belongs properly to the biographer and historian and not to the literary critic. He did not, of course, stop writing; but the days of his genuine creativity were gone. He continued to publish widely in periodicals and even continued lecturing, though he remained well within the borders of the South. In Charleston he played Dr. Johnson at Russell's bookstore to an admiring gathering of younger Southern authors, among them the poets Paul Hamilton Hayne and Henry Timrod. And in 1859 he published what was to be the final romance to appear in book form, *The Cassique of Kiawah.*

The Cassique, not included in later reprints of the Redfield edition and hence little known even to the readers of that massive collection, is an odd work in several respects. A story of Indian warfare and piratical adventures at sea, it is mainly set in the colonial South Carolina region of the late seventeenth century. But though its scene is the familiar one of the Revolutionary tales and though some of its incidents have parallels with these earlier stories, it is closer in mood to the Spanish romances. It was, evidently, a subject that Simms had long contemplated, and he may have written some portions of it as early as 1845.[7] It has its exciting moments, but in general its atmosphere is unusually dreamlike and its heroine springs straight from a wish-fulfillment fantasy. Simms was being sorely tried in this year of 1859. His plantation was a financial drain, and he had recently lost two young sons to the yellow fever; perhaps he hoped to escape into a romantic past far away from the grim present. He himself was to consider *The Cassique* one of his best romances (*L,* V, 241). He may have felt that it added yet another epoch to his local history; but it contributed little besides historical background to the mythical South of the Revolutionary and border tales.

With the opening of the Civil War—fittingly, he himself witnessed the firing on Fort Sumter—Simms devoted much energy to the Confederate cause.[8] He had increasingly accepted battle as probable; and, in letters to Hammond and others, he had discussed the economic and military potentials of both sides with skill and insight. During the early years of the war he was certain that the South would triumph; at the very least it would win independence from a North debilitated by internal corruption and disorder. As he wrote his New York friend Lawson in August, 1861, "Every battle, thus far, has resulted in a Southern victory. . . . Your Generals are cashiered. Your army demoralized." He could even be slightly patronizing: "Of all this, you, among others, were well warned long ago. I do not blame *you* for this war. I know that you desired peace" (*L*, IV, 373-74). A few months later he was still sanguine: "We are now *living* the first grand epic of our newly-born Confederacy. We are *making* the materials for the drama, and for future songs and fiction . . ." (*L*, IV, 413).

But the inevitable plunge in Simms's hopes was soon to come. Shortly after he had buried yet another of his children, his beloved plantation house burned down, apparently as the result of an accident.[9] It is a measure of the high regard in which he was held that the people of South Carolina, by public subscription, contributed a fund toward its rebuilding. This mark of affection was the only really bright spot in these dismal years. In 1863 his wife died unexpectedly, and grief over her loss made him ill for weeks; later, his son Gilmore was wounded in the fighting in Virginia. All these events were but part of the hardships of many Southerners during the war, and he met them with fortitude. But Simms was to be personally tried more than most men of his age. In 1865 stragglers trailing General Sherman's army put the torch to "Woodlands," and this time he suffered the loss of the wing housing his ten-thousand volume library. It was a symbolic act for an invading enemy, for in his collection were some of the works he had consulted while writing his Revolutionary romances. And now the wrong side had won; in the ashes of "Woodlands" lay the fabric of his dream of an ideal Southern nation.

But if the dream was ended, hard reality remained after Appomattox; and Simms drove on with courage, if not with optimism. After the restoration of peace, he immediately renewed contact with old friends in the North; and, as if he were a youth, he set out again to woo editors in New York to accept a new flood of poems, stories, articles, and reviews. He collected and edited a volume of war poetry of the South; he published his eyewitness account of the burning of Columbia, South Carolina; he tried anything in the effort to support his still large family and to rebuild his ruined estate.

Simms's final long works of fiction were three romances published in serial form in 1867 and in 1869. The first of these, "Joscelyn," was another Revolutionary tale, with a Georgia setting; it was not a new idea, since he had collected materials for it as early as 1858.[10] The other two—"The Cub of the Panther" and "Voltmeier"—are both laid in the border regions of the Carolinas.[11] All three tales have remained buried in obscure periodicals, and they have been little known. Trent, who dug them out, thought that "The Cub of the Panther" showed a new realistic and anti-romantic vein;[12] "Voltmeier," printed in the same year, is more in the old spirit of the border romances. The subject of one other unpublished late work is unknown; but, since Simms had spoken of the French and Indian Wars and of Texas and Mexico as potential topics, it was perhaps one of these.

As his letters of the late 1860's attest, Simms's distress of mind and body was acute during this last period of composition. Such a welter of activity could scarcely have produced much of permanent value, even if he had been a greater artist. As it was, he was grateful that his pen could help supply him with the bare necessities which others in the devastated South had no means of obtaining. Nowhere are his spirit and his resourcefulness better exemplified than in a letter to E. A. Duyckinck written while he was in New York dickering with publishers. He closed it thus:

> What I write here, & now, must needs be short & desultory. And while here, my object is to make such arrangements for permanent writing as will enable me to return to Woodlands, in the autumn, with full & regular employment on hand to exercise my pen all the winter. I propose, if possible, to concentrate myself this winter on a romance, and on "My Life and Times, an Autobiography, and a History." I have personally known a large number of the chief men of the South, for the last forty years; have been ruined, as a Union Man, by Nullification, and more lately by Secession; & have to commence life *de novo*, but with youth gone, and with young children looking to me for the wherewithall of life. Of all that I had; slaves, stocks, furniture, books, pictures, horses, mules, carriages, &c.—a property which was worth $150,000 in gold—I have nothing left me but my Lands, and these so long as we shall lack labour, must remain comparatively valueless. But, we must strive, not whine. Thanks,— & God be with you in mercy [*L*, IV, 577].

Simms, too, needed God's mercy, and in a sense he received it. With nearly all that he loved now gone, his constant and brain-wearying labor at least kept him from despondent regret over the stark fact that for the South of his old vision there was no future. On May 3, 1870, he was invited to make the opening address at a floral fair in the city in which he had been born, and he received an ovation. Just a few weeks later he was dead.

III *The Achievement of Simms*

Twenty-two years after the death of Simms, his biographer, Trent, asserted that at the close of his career he "was beginning to realize that the day of the romancer was over, and that that of the realist was dawning."[13] Like many a good nineteenth-century progressivist, Trent saw the history of literature in evolutionary terms: romance had flourished and died and now it was the turn of realism to rise beyond it. The analogy is, of course, false. Literature does not climb up a spiral toward ideal forms; rather, if we must speak of it in spatial terms, it may be figured as a network, with no absolute center and with its threads creeping off in many directions.

It is important to recognize this fact if one is to make any just evaluation of the worth of Simms's fiction. For it has long been the tendency of critics to treat the historical romance as a primitive and discredited genre. Critics have learned, during the so-called "realistic" period, to laugh at the romance's wooden protagonists, at its stock plot devices, at its turgid rhetoric, at its "unreal" view of life. And so it has been comparatively easy to classify Simms: He drew his commonplace romantic elements from Scott, Cooper, and a host of others; at his best, he was only a minor imitator. Occasionally, it is sometimes added, his "strong instinct for reality" (the phrase is Parrington's) did prevail and drove him to portray the "actuality" around him. He was finally, then, critics say, a "romantic realist," a "realistic romancer"—in short, neither one nor the other, an unstable writer who never resolved his dilemma.

It is not difficult to make out this sort of unfavorable case against Simms. Certainly he took little care to give his works polish; as his friends were always telling him, he wrote too often and entered too many fields to allow his talents full development in any. He was consistently wrongheaded in his view of himself as essentially a poet and playwright who had to get himself "on record" (*L*, III, 127) so that posterity could properly evaluate his claims. He was no great creator of individual character; of all his personages, not even Porgy remains long in the memory of the reader of a number of his romances. His plots are indeed hackneyed, derivative, repetitive, overly sensational. He was restrained by the conventions which popular taste imposed upon the fiction of his day, and he made no real effort to break those bonds. He was too contented with the near-word, with the cliché; and his sentences, jotted down at top speed, often became hopelessly tangled.

All these strictures are true, and one would not argue that Simms deserves any higher rank among the craftsmen of fiction than he has been awarded in the past. But another and less severe case could be made from these same facts, if one were to relate them to Simms's own concept of the romance's basic purposes. He once wrote another literary man, E. A. Duyckinck, "In proportion as a man is imaginative is he *original,* and originality is the main secret of vitality" (*L,* III, 388). Simms was not concerned, that is, so much with the structure and style of his tales as he was with the ideas which he trusted they would convey. Originality and vitality were to him more desirable than shape and finish. He therefore chose, quite consciously, the freer form of the romance—with its representative characters, its panoramic sweep, its violent contrasts between disorder and unity—as the vehicle for rendering his original vision of an essential South in the process of development.

At his best, then, Simms was concerned with a theme; and this study submits that it is this theme alone that makes a body of his fiction worthy of attention today. The only wide-ranging imaginative account of ante-bellum Southern society recorded by an acute and talented observer, it stands as a unique cultural document. Whatever one may personally feel about that society, it would seem to deserve at least the sort of explication which has already been given to the myth of the western-story West. This study has tried to demonstrate that Simms was most successful as a writer when he was most implicated in his own legend of the South; when he strayed from it, as in his Spanish romances and "psychological" novels, he wrote without real conviction. He needed exuberance, passion, intense involvement to create a living story, and his burning desire to see the South lead all societies on earth into the future provided him with that drive.

It was the *ideal*, it must be reiterated, that motivated his best work; he saw an unprecedented community rising in a colonial and heroic period and passing through severe trials *toward* order and stability. He had re-created a past for his South from which it could draw virtue and courage, but in his fictional portrayal he did not insist that complete perfection had yet been attained. Certainly he was most convincing in this literary role; as the Civil War neared, he diverted his talents to more strident defense of Southern institutions and he blurred his own critical recognition of still prevalent weaknesses.

As the reader knows, the myth of Southern perfectibility which Simms shared with many of his compatriots was to lead to disaster. It was indeed a dangerous form of self-deception that Southerners had lost themselves in by 1860. But, as one historian has commented, "Even though the idealized portrait of the South was false, it was to be a strong and living force in the years ahead. In the long run, the vision of the perfect South was to supply a substantial element in the construction of the romantic legend about the Old South. In the nearer future, it was to give the Confederate soldier something to die for."[14]

And, it might be added, in the farther future it was again to provide a powerful stimulus to such writers of the South as William Faulkner and Robert Penn Warren. This is not a suggestion that these authors have drawn directly from knowledge of Simms's work. But surely Simms's portraits of the old aristocrat, the common-sensical frontiersman, the young hothead, the self-seeking poor white, helped to fix these archetypal figures in the Southern consciousness. Certainly better than any other creative writer of his era and region he managed to capture the essence of the Old South dream.

When Simms was yet a young man thinking about the failures and successes of his early volumes of poetry, he prayed that he would be given the power to celebrate the South in truly epic fashion. His course as an author was to take him into many strange byways and up several blind alleys, but to the end of his career he was constant in that desire. And, more often than has been recognized, his prayer was granted.

Notes and References

Chapter One

1. *The Letters of William Gilmore Simms,* eds. Mary C. Simms Oliphant, Alfred Taylor Odell, T. C. Duncan Eaves (Columbia, S. C., 1952), I, 159. This edition hereafter abbreviated in text and notes as *L.* Biographical material in this section is based largely on the introductory sketch by A. S. Salley in *L,* I, lix-lxxxix.

2. William P. Trent, *William Gilmore Simms* (Boston, 1892), pp. 8-9. Hereafter referred to as Trent. See also *L,* I, lxii.

3. See John R. Welsh, "William Gilmore Simms, Critic of the South," *Journal of Southern History,* XXVI (May, 1960), 201-14.

4. *Southern Literary Messenger,* III (November, 1837), 641-57. References in text are to this version. The essay was reprinted as a pamphlet, *Slavery in America* (Richmond, 1838), and in slightly revised form in a symposium, *The Pro-Slavery Argument* (Charleston, 1852).

5. See, for example, *L,* II, 220-33, where he spoke of classifying his fiction as the "moral imaginative" (works like *Martin Faber*), the "border domestic," the "historical romance," and the "Revolutionary novels."

6. For further discussion of Tucker and of the other writers mentioned in this section, see Jay B. Hubbell, *The South in American Literature, 1607-1900* (Durham, 1954). I am indebted to Hubbell for a number of points. See also Alexander Cowie, *The Rise of the American Novel* (New York, 1948).

7. See Hubbell, *op. cit.,* pp. 492 ff., and *L,* I, 68.

8. Simms's views on the relationship between a national and a sectional literature are best expressed in his preface to *The Wigwam and the Cabin* (New York, 1856): "One word for the material of these legends. It is local, sectional—and to be *national* in literature, one must needs be *sectional.* No one mind can fully or fairly illustrate the characteristics of any great country; and he who shall depict *one section* faithfully, has made his proper and sufficient contribution to the great work of *national* illustration" (p. 4).

Chapter Two

1. *The Yemassee* (New York, 1835), I, vi-vii. Simms reprinted this passage in the preface to the revised edition (New York, 1853).

2. William Congreve had noted the difference as early as 1692,

in the preface to his *Incognita;* and later writers such as Clara Reeve, Sir Walter Scott, Cooper, and—notably—Hawthorne, had carried on the discussion. For recent treatments of the subject, from which I have drawn, see: Richard Chase, *The American Novel and Its Tradition* (New York, 1957); Leslie Fiedler, *Love and Death in the American Novel* (New York, 1960); and Daniel G. Hoffman, *Form and Fable in American Fiction* (New York, 1961).

3. I am speaking, of course, essentially of the *popular* romance and not of the complex and ambivalent works of writers like Melville and Hawthorne who moved far beyond the usual type.

4. Relevant source and influence studies are: C. Hugh Holman, "The Influence of Scott and Cooper on Simms," *American Literature,* XXIII (May, 1951), 203-18; J. Wesley Thomas, "The German Sources of William Gilmore Simms," *Anglo-German and American-German Crosscurrents,* I (1957), 127-53; C. Hugh Holman, "Simms and the British Dramatists," *PMLA,* LXV (June, 1950), 346-59. See also G. Harrison Orians, "The Romance Ferment After *Waverley,*" *American Literature,* III (January, 1932), 408-31; Grace Landrum, "Scott and his Literary Rivals in the Old South," *American Literature,* II (November, 1930), 256-76; and Stanley T. Williams, *The Spanish Background of American Literature* (New Haven, 1955). A review of Simms's own attitudes toward fiction is in Edd W. Parks, *William Gilmore Simms as Literary Critic* (Athens, Ga., 1961). A useful compilation of critical theories about fiction is in William Charvat, *The Origins of American Critical Thought, 1810-1835* (Philadelphia, 1936).

5. *Views and Reviews, First Series* (New York, 1845), p. 219.

6. The review is quoted in part in *L*, I, 152 ff.

Chapter Three

1. These volumes are: *Monody on the Death of Gen. Charles Cotesworth Pinckney* (Charleston, 1825); *Lyrical and Other Poems* (Charleston, 1827); *Early Lays* (Charleston, 1827); *The Vision of Cortes* (Charleston, 1829); *The Tri-Color* (London, 1830); *Atalantis* (New York, 1832).

2. New York, 1833; reference in text to this edition. It was republished in 1837 with the addition of several short tales that had seen magazine publication. *Martin Faber* itself was reworked from a magazine story published in 1829.

3. *Guy Rivers* (New York, 1834), p. viii. Further references are to the revised edition (New York, 1855) and are incorporated in the

text. Simms notes in the preface to this latter edition that he had written part of the story—undoubtedly that dealing with Guy Rivers himself—several years earlier. See also *L*, II, 224-25.

4. These and other quotations from contemporary reviews are in *L*, I, 59-61; II, 225-27.

5. For example, Albert Keiser, in *The Indian in American Literature* (New York, 1933), p. 154, calls Simms's treatment "One of the most faithful portraits of the American native."

6. *The Yemassee* (New York, 1853), p. 297. Further references to this edition incorporated in text.

7. Because of the continuing popularity of *The Yemassee* over all the rest of Simms's fiction, a good bit of scholarship has been devoted to his treatment of Indian character—especially in comparison with Cooper's. But it ought to be understood that the Indian as a major character figures only in *The Yemassee, The Cassique of Kiawah*, and some of the shorter tales. Simms created no character like Cooper's Chingachgook, to be carried through several books.

8. As Donald Davidson comments (*L*, I, xlii), such characters prefigure the Sartorises in the novels of Faulkner. Some of Simms's poor-whites are also recognizably ante-bellum Snopeses. I have found Davidson's comments generally useful.

Chapter Four

1. Quotations from reviews can be found in *L*, I, 63, 71; II, 226-28.

2. Use of the American Revolution as a subject for fiction was not new. Among the earlier authors who had treated some phase of it were Cooper and Lydia Maria Child; Catharine M. Sedgwick and John Pendleton Kennedy published works dealing with the war in the same year as *The Partisan*. Simms was, however, the first fiction writer to present a detailed account of the whole Southern campaign.

3. *The Partisan* (New York, 1854), p. vii. Further references to this edition incorporated in text.

4. There is probably an autobiographical element in Simms's creation of the character of Emily Singleton. His first wife had died of consumption after a long illness only three years before.

5. See, for example, H. M. Jarrell, "Falstaff and Simms's Porgy," *American Literature*, III (May, 1931), 204-12. See also C. Hugh Holman "Simms and the British Dramatists," *PMLA*, LXV (June, 1950), 346-59. Edward P. Vandiver, Jr., in "Simms's Porgy and Cooper," *Modern Language Notes*, LXX (April, 1955), 272-74, argues

for similarities between Porgy and Cooper's Captain Lawton and Captain Polwarth.

6. Trent, p. 109, says: "I have it on good authority that he intended Porgy to be a reproduction of himself in certain moods."

7. *Southern Literary Messenger*, II (January, 1836), 117-21.

Chapter Five

1. *Mellichampe* (New York, 1854), pp. 4-5. Further references to this edition incorporated in text.

2. Simms wrote Lawson just before *Mellichampe* appeared: "[Y]ou have no idea how popular Porgy is with a large majority. He is actually the founder of a sect" (*L*, I, 82).

3. John W. Higham, in "The Changing Loyalties of William Gilmore Simms," *Journal of Southern History*, IX (May, 1943), 210-23, has seen this marriage as causing Simms to switch from commercial views to those of the landed class. A. S. Salley, however, argues (*L*, I, lxxxvi) that Simms had himself been a landholder and slaveowner and that the only real change was that he thereafter spent more time on the plantation and less in the city. Simms's ideas as expressed in his fiction before his marriage support Salley's conclusions. William Cullen Bryant, one of the many literary figures Simms entertained at "Woodlands," described it in *Homes of American Authors* (New York, 1853). The plantation, incidentally, is still in existence.

4. *Pelayo* was published in 1838; *Count Julian,* the manuscript of which was mislaid for a period, did not appear until 1845. See *L*, IV, 595, n. 208.

5. Trent, p. 112.

6. *Richard Hurdis* (New York, 1855), p. 11. Further references to this edition incorporated in the text. Simms also issued a collection of his shorter fiction, *Carl Werner*, this same year of 1838. *Richard Hurdis, Border Beagles,* and *Beauchampe,* incidentally, were first published anonymously; Simms wished, so wrote a friend, "to try an experiment upon the critics" (*L*, I, 299).

7. F. H. Deen, in "A Comparison of Simms's *Richard Hurdis* with its Sources," *Modern Language Notes*, LX (June, 1945), 406-8, cites the chief works consulted and concludes: "It is only in a very general way that Simms follows the available source material."

8. Simms made a similar point in an essay on Southern literature written late in 1840. See *L*, I, 206-7.

9. See discussion in Chapter II.

Chapter Six

1. *The Scout* (New York, 1854), pp. 140-43. The original title under which the book appeared was *The Kinsmen* (Philadelphia, 1841). The change of title for the Redfield edition indicates that Simms realized that the story's true center is not the fight between the "kinsmen" but Jack Bannister himself.

2. *Confession* (New York, 1856), p. 7.

3. *Beauchampe; or the Kentucky Tragedy* was originally published in Philadelphia in 1842. Simms later reworked the first part of the narrative and issued it as *Charlemont* (New York, 1856). The second half he also altered and republished the same year under the original title *Beauchampe*. This process has confused many of Simms's commentators, including Trent. The "Kentucky tragedy" itself has had a surprisingly lively history in American literature. With varying degrees of fidelity to the facts as known, the story has been used (among others) by Poe in *Politian*, Thomas Holley Chivers in two plays, and Charles Fenno Hoffman in *Grayslaer*. The most recent (and notable) version is Robert Penn Warren's *World Enough and Time* (New York, 1950).

For a discussion of the case and treatments of it see Willard Jillson, "The Beauchamp-Sharp Tragedy in American Literature," *Register of Kentucky State Historical Society*, XXXVI (1938), 54-60. W. B. Gates, in "William Gilmore Simms and the Kentucky Tragedy," *American Literature*, XXXII (May, 1960), 158-66, points out Simms's borrowings from Elizabethan drama and Milton, argues that *Charlemont* and *Beauchampe* are not mere transcriptions of the real event, and passes the judgment (which I cannot share) that they "are not entirely lacking in art." Simms himself once called *Beauchampe* "the best" of the border romances (*L*, I, 339).

4. Simms's talents found better expression in the expanded romance than in the shorter tale, where he often relied too heavily on German models. Nevertheless, a few of his short stories still have interest—particularly "Grayling," a work that Poe praised highly. Late in life, Simms revealingly remarked, "The degree & kind of invention necessary to a *short* story are far greater than in a long one" (*L*, V, 77). See J. Allen Morris, "The Short Stories of William Gilmore Simms," *American Literature*, XIV (March, 1942), 20-35.

5. Simms's career as editor is necessarily beyond the scope of this study. For further information see William S. Hoole, "William Gilmore Simms's Career as Editor," *Georgia Historical Quarterly*, XIX (March, 1936), 47-54; and Edd W. Parks, *William Gilmore Simms as Literary Critic* (Athens, Ga., 1961).

Chapter Seven

1. *Katharine Walton* (New York, 1854), p. 353. Further references to this edition incorporated in text. In serial form the story had appeared in *Godey's,* February-December, 1850.

2. For a fuller discussion of Simms and *Uncle Tom's Cabin* see S. P. C. Duvall, "W. G. Simms's Review of Mrs. Stowe," *American Literature,* XXX (March, 1958), 107-17; and my reply to this article, "*Woodcraft:* Simms's First Answer to *Uncle Tom's Cabin,*" *American Literature,* XXXI (January, 1960), 421-33. Some material in this chapter is drawn from the latter article. Trent says that Simms assigned Louisa S. Cheves McCord to do the review of *Uncle Tom's Cabin* in the *Southern Quarterly Review* because he preferred "the seemingly poetic justice of having the Northern woman answered by a Southern woman" (pp. 174-75). *Woodcraft* was first issued in book form as *The Sword and the Distaff* (Charleston, 1852) after appearing in serial form in the *Southern Literary Gazette;* as part of the Redfield edition it was slightly revised and reissued in 1854 under the new (and really less relevant) title of *Woodcraft, or, Hawks about the Dovecote.* All page references are to this latter edition, which is more easily available; and I have chosen to refer to the book by its more familiar title. Simms mentioned *Uncle Tom's Cabin* in a revised version of his review of Harriet Martineau which appeared in *The Pro-Slavery Argument* (Charleston, 1852). The preface to this review is dated July 1, 1852, so he had definitely read *Uncle Tom's Cabin* before this date—and while his own new romance was still appearing in serial parts.

3. Donald Davidson makes this point in *L,* I, xlv. The passage, incidentally, sounds startlingly like descriptions of Confederate soldiers returning to their homes.

4. Simms talked about a sequel to *Woodcraft* in which Porgy was "to become a Legislator" (*L,* IV, 168). The book was never written.

Chapter Eight

1. *Southward Ho!* (New York, 1854), pp. 254-55. The novelist John Esten Cooke, reviewing the book for the *Southern Literary Messenger,* concluded: "the best criticism of this entertaining volume would be the simple declaration that every thing about it is *Southern*" (Quoted in *L,* III, 355).

2. *The Forayers* (New York, 1855), p. 5; hereafter abbreviated in text as *F,* with citations to this edition. *Eutaw* (New York, 1856) will be cited as *E* in references.

3. In *L*, III, 405 and 423, Simms speaks of possible treatments of the battles of King's Mountain and Gum Swamp. In his last years he returned to the Revolution in stories that received serial publication only. These latter tales are discussed in Chapter IX.

4. For Simms's interest in spiritualism and clairvoyance, including an account of séances he attended in New York, see *L*, III, 475 ff.

Chapter Nine

1. The new editions of his earlier works drew many flattering retrospective accounts both in Northern and Southern periodicals. For extracts from reviews, see *L*, III, *passim*. Several of Simms's books, incidentally, also achieved English and German editions.

2. For these and other titles, see *L*, III, 437.

3. Evert A. and George Duyckinck published their monumental *Cyclopaedia of American Literature* in 1855. Simms contributed many of the facts about Southern letters; see *L*, III, *passim*, for the rough notes which he forwarded.

4. *L*, III, 521. The lecture is reprinted as an appendix to this volume; further references incorporated in text. Simms had replied to earlier Northern treatments of South Carolina's role in the *Southern Quarterly Review*, XIV (July, 1848), 37-44.

5. Charles S. Sydnor, *The Development of Southern Sectionalism, 1819-1848* (Baton Rouge, 1948), p. 338.

6. Several reviews of the lecture are quoted in *L*, III, 456 ff.

7. See *L*, II, 81. In *L*, I, 285, he says he had written part of a novel on the same subject when he was in his late teens.

8. See *L*, IV, 355. The letters of the war years are a valuable contribution to the history of the Confederacy as seen by an articulate and by no means uncritical observer.

9. See *L*, IV, 399. His Charleston house had burned in 1860.

10. See *L*, IV, 41. The letters of the 1860's have occasional references to various subjects for projected new works of fiction.

11. "Joscelyn" was published in the *Old Guard*, January-December, 1867; Simms apparently planned to revise it for book publication. "The Cub of the Panther" appeared in the *Old Guard*, January-December, 1869; and "Voltmeier, or the Mountain Men" in the *Illuminated Western World*, March-July, 1869. One other long tale, "Paddy McGann; or, the Demon of the Stump," had been serialized in the *Southern Illustrated News*, February-May, 1863.

12. See Trent, pp. 314 ff.

13. *Ibid.*, p. 315.

14. Sydnor, *op. cit.*, p. 339.

Selected Bibliography

PRIMARY SOURCES

Simms published more than eighty volumes in several different fields. Listed below are the first editions of the most important works of fiction and a representative sampling of his other work. There are at present modern editions of *Woodcraft* and *The Yemassee* only.

Fiction

Beauchampe. Philadelphia: Lea & Blanchard, 1842; New York: Redfield, 1856 (rev. ed.).
Border Beagles. Philadelphia: Carey & Hart, 1840.
The Cassique of Kiawah. New York: Redfield, 1859.
Charlemont. New York: Redfield, 1856.
Confession. Philadelphia: Lea & Blanchard, 1841.
Eutaw. New York: Redfield, 1856.
The Forayers. New York: Redfield, 1855.
Guy Rivers. New York: Harper & Brothers, 1834.
Katharine Walton. Philadelphia: A. Hart, 1851.
The Kinsmen. Philadelphia, Lea & Blanchard, 1841. (Later retitled *The Scout*, New York: Redfield, 1854.)
Mellichampe. New York: Harper & Bros., 1836.
The Partisan. New York: Harper & Bros., 1835.
Richard Hurdis. Philadelphia: Carey & Hart, 1838.
Southward Ho! New York: Redfield, 1854.
The Sword and the Distaff. Charleston: Walker, Richards & Co., 1852. (Later retitled *Woodcraft*, New York: Redfield, 1854; modern reprint of this edition, New York: W. W. Norton & Co., 1961.)
Vasconselos. New York: Redfield, 1853.
The Wigwam and the Cabin. New York: Wiley & Putnam, 1845.
The Yemassee. New York: Harper & Bros., 1835. (Modern editions: New York: American Book Co., 1937; New York: Twayne Publishers, Inc., 1962.)

Poetry

Poems Descriptive, Dramatic, Legendary and Contemplative. New York: Redfield, 1853.

Essays

Views and Reviews in American Literature, History and Fiction. New York: Wiley & Putnam, 1845.

Biography

The Life of Francis Marion. New York: Henry G. Langley, 1844.

Miscellaneous

The Geography of South Carolina. Charleston: Babcock & Co., 1843.
The History of South Carolina. Charleston: Babcock & Co., 1840.

Letters

The Letters of William Gilmore Simms. Eds. Mary C. Simms Oliphant,
Alfred Taylor Odell, T. C. Duncan Eaves. Columbia: University
of South Carolina Press, 1952-1956. 5 vols. Carefully edited
texts and an indispensable critical apparatus, including one of
the fullest listings of Simms's periodical writings. The introduction
by Donald Davidson and the biographical sketch by A. S. Salley
are valuable.

Collected Edition

In the 1850's the New York publisher J. S. Redfield (and, later, his
successor W. J. Widdleton) published the only collection of Simms's
writings. This included those works listed above under *Fiction* and
Poetry. Illustrations were by F. O. C. Darley. The stereotype plates
were used for many reprintings duing the remainder of the nineteenth century. Many large libraries have either the original or a
reprint of this set, which contains Simms's own selection and revision
of his best fiction.

Bibliography

A. S. SALLEY. *Catalogue of the Salley Collection of the Works of
William Gilmore Simms.* Columbia, S.C.: Printed for the author,
1943. The most complete descriptive bibliography of books by
Simms.

SECONDARY SOURCES

Books

Most of the work on Simms so far exists in the form of unpublished
doctoral dissertations. A new biography is greatly needed.

BROOKS, VAN WYCK. *The World of Washington Irving.* New York:
E. P. Dutton & Co., 1944. Contains an impressionistic and
somewhat inaccurate picture of Simms's milieu.
COWIE, ALEXANDER. *The Rise of the American Novel.* New York:

American Book Co., 1948. Includes an extended examination of Simms, some of it drawn from Cowie's introduction to the 1937 edition of *The Yemassee*.

HUBBELL, JAY B. *The South in American Literature, 1607-1900.* Durham: Duke University Press, 1954. In a lengthy analysis of Simms, Hubbell puts him in the context of the Old South and of national letters.

LEISY, ERNEST E. *The American Historical Novel.* Norman: University of Oklahoma Press, 1950. Useful for a comparison of Simms's romances with works of other writers on the same historical subjects.

PARKS, EDD W. *William Gilmore Simms as Literary Critic.* Athens: University of Georgia Press, 1961. The fullest compilation of Simms's critical views on a variety of topics.

PARRINGTON, VERNON L. *Main Currents in American Thought.* New York: Harcourt Brace & Co., 1927. Vol. II. A thoroughgoing critical evaluation of Simms that insists upon seeing him as a natural realist who was frustrated by a romantic Southern environment.

TAYLOR, WILLIAM R. *Cavalier and Yankee.* New York: George Braziller, 1961. Discusses the development of the antipodal myths of the "Cavalier" of the South and the "Yankee"; has interesting things to say about Simms's contributions to the process.

TRENT, WILLIAM P. *William Gilmore Simms.* American Men of Letters. Boston: Houghton, Mifflin & Co., 1892. Still the only full-length life to see print, this work is marred by Trent's hatred for everything Simms's Old South stood for. Does contain some documentary material not available elsewhere. A valuable corrective is A. S. Salley's sketch of Simms's life in Volume I of the *Letters*.

Essays

Many of the periodical articles on Simms are concerned with sources or with minor points in single works. For full listings see Lewis Leary, *Articles on American Literature, 1900-1950* (Durham, N.C.: Duke University Press, 1954) and, since 1950, the bibliographies in the journals *PMLA* and *American Literature*. Listed below are some studies of general interest. (A few others not listed here are discussed in the notes and references section.)

DUVALL, S. P. C. "W. G. Simms's Review of Mrs. Stowe," *American Literature*, XXX (March, 1958), 107-17. Argues that Simms retorted to Mrs. Stowe in an unsigned review of *A Key to Uncle Tom's Cabin* in the *Southern Quarterly Review* for July, 1853.

Selected Bibliography

GUILDS, JOHN C. "Simms's Views on National and Sectional Literature, 1825-1845," *North Carolina Historical Review*, XXXIV (July, 1957), 393-405. Analyzes Simms's view that to be national a literature must be sectional first.

HIGHAM, JOHN W. "The Changing Loyalties of William Gilmore Simms," *Journal of Southern History*, IX (May, 1943), 210-23. Tries to show that Simms's views about the South underwent a change after he married into a plantation-owning family.

HOLMAN, C. HUGH. "Simms and the British Dramatists," *PMLA*, LXV (June, 1950), 346-59. Discusses the influence of Simms's wide reading in the drama on his handling of plot and character in his fiction.

————. "The Influence of Scott and Cooper on Simms," *American Literature*, XXIII (May, 1951), 203-18. A discussion of Simms's debts to two of his predecessors in the historical romance.

————. "William Gilmore Simms's Picture of the Revolution as a Civil Conflict," *Journal of Southern History*, XV (November, 1949), 441-62. Useful for its analysis of Simms's historical attitudes in his Revolutionary romances.

MORRIS, J. ALLEN. "The Stories of William Gilmore Simms," *American Literature*, XIV (March, 1942), 20-35. Lists chronologically fifty-eight tales.

RIDGELY, JOSEPH V. "*Woodcraft*: Simms's First Answer to *Uncle Tom's Cabin*," *American Literature*, XXXI (January, 1960), 421-33. Replies to Duvall (see above) and argues that Simms's first retort to Mrs. Stowe was through the medium of a work of fiction published before the *Southern Quarterly Review* notice.

THOMAS, J. WESLEY. "The German Sources of William Gilmore Simms," *Anglo-German and American-German Crosscurrents*, I (1957), 127-53. Valuable for its demonstration of Simms's specific knowledge of German literature. Notes particularly German influence on the short tales and on six of the longer romances.

VANDIVER, EDWARD P., JR. "Simms's Border Romances and Shakespeare," *Shakespeare Quarterly*, V (April, 1954), 129-39. Cites Simms's acquaintance with Shakespeare's works and shows how he absorbed the Elizabethan love of violence, emotion, and imaginative fancy into his fiction.

WELSH, JOHN R. "William Gilmore Simms, Critic of the South," *Journal of Southern History*, XXVI (May, 1960), 201-14. Finds that Simms was critical of the South in three chief areas: it was intellectually lazy; it was agriculturally deficient; it was economically weak.

Index